Plato & Aristotle

Philosophy of Religion Coursebook

Stephen Loxton

Published by Inducit Learning Ltd trading as pushmepress.com,

Pawlett House, West Street, Somerton,

Somerset TA11 7PS, United Kingdom

www.pushmepress.com

First published in 2013

ISBN: 978-1-909618-40-4

Links, reviews, news and revision materials available on

www.philosophicalinvestigations.co.uk

With over 20,000 visitors a month, the philosophical investigations website allows students and teachers to explore Philosophy of Religion and Ethics through handouts, film clips, presentations, case studies, extracts, games and academic articles.

Pitched just right, and so much more than a text book, here is a place to engage with critical reflection whatever your level. Marked student essays are also posted.

Contents

Introduction

This book aims to provide a guide to the key themes and theories of Plato (427-347 BCE) and Aristotle (384-322 BCE) as set for study within the OCR's GCE A-level in Religious Studies OCR (G571).

Within the OCR Specification the topics to review are listed under the title 'Ancient Greek influences on philosophy of religion'. Plato and Aristotle's thought is to be studied, with reference to ideas in Plato's Republic (Book VII: 514a - 521b) and Aristotle's Metaphysics (Book 12). First-hand knowledge of the texts is, however, 'not expected'. Candidates are expected to 'be able to highlight the strengths and weaknesses' of Plato and Aristotle's ideas with regard to the following topics and themes:

- **PLATO** - to demonstrate knowledge and understanding of what might be represented in the Analogy of the Cave by 'the prisoners, the shadows, the cave itself, the outside world, the sun, the journey out of the cave and the return to the prisoners'. (By 'analogy' here, we mean how one thing might be taken to correspond to, or be like, another). Additionally Plato's 'concept of the Forms' and 'the Form of the Good' are set, so candidates 'should understand what Plato meant by 'Forms' and be able to demonstrate knowledge and understanding of the relation between concepts and phenomena, the concept of 'Ideals', and the relation between the Form of the Good and the other Forms'.

- **ARISTOTLE** - the specification specifies 'ideas about cause and purpose in relation to God'; 'Aristotle's understanding of material, efficient, formal and final cause'; and 'Aristotle's concept of the Prime Mover.'

With all of the ideas the challenge is that 'Candidates should be able to discuss critically the validity of the above points'.

The details here will be unpacked and reviewed shortly, but a question arising might be that of wondering why a study of Plato and Aristotle has been set. A good answer to this question comes from the philosopher Anthony Kenny who recently wrote that, 'The works of Aristotle and his master Plato provide a paradigm of philosophy for every age, and to this day anyone using the title "philosopher" is claiming to be one of their heirs.' (Kenny 2010 p.10)

Kenny uses the term 'paradigm' here, meaning that Plato and Aristotle give exemplary models of what it is to do philosophy. Scholars have been paying such tributes as this for the best part of two millennia. Even so, does it not strike us as odd that Greek philosophers from the classical period remain on the agenda today?

An answer to this is the suggestion that Plato faced 'essentially the same political, philosophical and religious problems as ourselves.' He lived in a time when systems of government were breaking down, when faith in institutions and progress was shaken. But in such a setting, in the literature of the time, and particularly the philosophical literature of Plato, there was an intellectual engagement with the issues and a thorough interrogation of the problems that had 'an intelligence, a freshness, and a vigour which will hardly be found in the same measure in any later literature.' (Lowes Dickenson 1947 p. viii)

We should not be in doubt that for the times we live in Plato (c. 427-347 BCE) and Aristotle (c. 384-322 BCE) are worth studying for the quality of their ideas and for what they demonstrate as the method and point of philosophy. On all these matters Plato and Aristotle remain instructive and influential.

In what follows Plato and Aristotle are key figures, but it is impossible to consider them without including Socrates (c. 468-399 BCE). To avoid confusion it is as well to know that sometime in the 410s Plato became a friend and student of Socrates. After Socrates' death Plato steadily moved towards an academic career and began to write play-like dialogues in which philosophical problems are explored by named characters in discussion. In his works Plato gives a leading role to the character 'Socrates', thus fusing a tribute to his revered teacher with a brilliantly conceived way of presenting his own ideas and concerns. From c.387 BCE Plato founded the Academy, a centre for academic study that can be regarded as the prototype of a university. Aristotle came to study there c.367. Thus Socrates taught and became a friend of Plato, and Plato taught and became a friend of Aristotle. However many disagreements we may note between the ideas of Plato and Aristotle, all the evidence is that they each had a high and positive regard for each other.

To provide a secure view of how the theories in the set works fit into the thought of Plato and Aristotle we will see how in the Meno Plato sets out an early approach to the idea of the form of the Good, and note some other ideas on the forms set out in Phaedo and Republic. Then we will consider two other similes (likenesses) or analogies from Republic, the Sun and the 'divided line'. In a similar way, Aristotle's ideas on intellectual methodology, matter and form, and the relation between actuality and potentiality will be examined as well as his ideas on the causes and the Prime Mover. In the final section of this book there is a review of a range of criticisms of Plato and Aristotle.

By way of a very brief preview some of the main ideas we will be considering include:

- Plato offers a type of 'dual aspect' view of reality: there is the visible, phenomenal world of change and sense, and an intelligible domain of general concepts, accessed by reason and within which the governing ideals or 'forms' have objective reality; the 'form of the Good' is the pre-eminent form.

- Aristotle thinks reality is eternal, but composed of matter that is in a continuous process of change in accordance with its nature or form. Change is a pattern of purposeful movement and it is caused by the lure of love generated by the Prime Mover. Change involves the actualisation of potential and has a four-fold character: material, formal, efficient and final.

Both Plato and Aristotle use the term 'form'. Plato's use of the term is especially important to our consideration of his philosophy. In the Greek Plato uses two words, **IDEA** and **EIDOS**, to mean the definitive meaning, truth, form, shape or pattern of the thing or concept in question. The Greek terms can be translated as 'form' or as 'idea'. The problem with 'idea' is that in English usage it tends to mean 'a person's ideas', namely, the idea or ideas a person may have 'in their mind.' By 'form' Plato never means an idea that is simply 'in the mind', so the term 'form' is much the better term to use. There will be much more to say about Plato's view of forms later, but here is one definition to consider:

> *'The forms are not mere concepts (hence the traditional alternative name "Ideas" is undesirable, as being misleading); they are ultimate facts, intelligible to our minds but quite independent of them. The things of our sensible world exist in a secondary sense, only in so far as they approximate to the corresponding form.' (H Tredennick, 1969:15)*

PLATO, ARISTOTLE AND THE SCHOOL OF ATHENS

Plato and Aristotle provide a foundation for much in the tradition of Western Philosophy and Christian Theology. Some insights into their significance can be found from a study of Raphael's painting of 1514, The School of Athens. We cannot reproduce the picture here, but illustrations relevant to this book will be found on the Philosophical Investigations website:

http://www.philosophicalinvestigations.co.uk/

In 1510, Raphael was commissioned by Pope Julius II to produce a series of frescos for his library. The four great realms of human knowledge, theology, philosophy, law and the arts were to be represented, and The School of Athens was Raphael's tribute to philosophy. The original is still in the Vatican.

There are three general points to make about the picture:

1. The setting of the picture is much more Rome than Athens. Raphael's setting is of a Roman basilica evoking St Peter's Cathedral, which was undergoing renovation at the time of the commission. Plato's Academy would not have had such spectacular architecture. Again, pictures of the archaeology in Athens of the site of the Academy are worth looking at via the website as above.

2. Raphael's picture is a tribute to the great tradition of Greek philosophy: within the picture, many of the revered figures from that tradition are shown in discussion irrespective of the fact that in real time most of them were not contemporaries.

3. The portrayal of philosophy as a process of active discussion is of

great importance, not least to Plato, for as we shall see later on, he is committed to the view that progress towards the truth on any matter comes primarily through discussion and not, to take a key alternative, through writing.

With these points in mind, and on the assumption that readers will be able to view the image online, let's analyse the picture.

We view the painting head-on, and in the centre, as in the detail, we have the figures of Plato, on the left, older and grey-haired, and Aristotle, on the right, the younger man. When Raphael painted the work he was determined to reflect the high level of regard in the period we now call the 'Renaissance' for classical thought and culture. To do justice to the key figures in the painting – those we see in the centre, in conversation and seemingly walking towards us, Raphael took as his model for Plato one of the greatest figures of his age, Leonardo da Vinci.

In the painting it looks as if Plato is in motion, walking forwards; he is carrying a copy of his work Timaeus, his most theological work as it happens and the most highly regarded of his works during the Renaissance. Plato is holding the book vertically, pointing upwards and matching his gesture as he points up. This represents his view that the everyday world of the here and the now is fleeting and partial, and dependent upon an eternal realm of concepts, the so-called 'world of forms'. To reinforce this, Raphael paints Plato's clothing in red and white to suggest the ethereal qualities of fire and air.

In contrast, Raphael paints Aristotle to be stationary; his feet are planted, he gestures down as if to indicate a commitment to this world and he is carrying a copy of his Nichomachean Ethics. Aristotle is shown carrying the book almost horizontally. This, plus Aristotle's gesture, signals his commitment to the immediate world of experience around us, thus representing the Aristotelian method of learning through a study of reality as we find it. Consistent with this, he is clothed in brown and blue to represent earth and water.

Raphael provides us with a kind of snapshot of the contrasting and complimentary philosophical styles of Plato and his most famous pupil Aristotle, and the pictures evokes the sense of philosophy as a process of discussion.

KEY TERMS

dialogue - simile - analogy - matter - form - actual - potential - change - paradigm

SELF-ASSESSMENT QUESTIONS

1. What is the historical relationship between Socrates and Plato?

2. What is the historical relationship between Plato and Aristotle?

3. Outline reasons why Plato and Aristotle are still important thinkers.

4. What are Plato's dialogues?

5. Why does Plato write in dialogues?

6. How does Plato think we best see reality?

7. How does Aristotle think we best see reality?

8. What so far does Plato seem to mean by 'forms'?

9. What so far does Aristotle think about change?

10. Look at 'The School of Athens' on the website (or via Google images): check if you can identify the points that illustrate the key ideas of Plato and Aristotle - check back with the text above afterwards.

FURTHER READING

- See the suggestions at the end of Chapter 2 for Plato and Chapter 3 on Aristotle. A good general guide is provided by Annas (2000).

Plato

PLATO'S WORLD

In the fifth century BCE Greece and the eastern Mediterranean was organised into a number of city-states. Athens, Thebes, Corinth and Sparta were prominent at the time of Plato, who grew up at a time when Athens had suffered a major setback. In 404 BCE Athens found itself on the losing side in the Peloponnesian war with Sparta that had lasted for some 27 years.

The Peloponnesian War (431–404 BCE) involved most of the Greek city-states who were arraigned in two alliances, one headed by Sparta and the other by Athens. The war had plenty of incidents and campaigns but crucially, in 405 a Spartan navy under the command of Lysander defeated the Athenian fleet at the battle of Aegopotami. This meant that the Spartans could blockade Athens and force surrender.

This led to savage times. The system of democracy Athens had introduced in 508 BCE was replaced by a group set up by the Spartan's to rule. They became known as the 'Thirty Tyrants' so severe were they. In 401 BCE the democracy was re-established, but as the democracy had lost the war and as Athens was now a weaker state, the prevalent mood was uncertainty. This was enough to get a thoughtful and intelligent person like Plato to ask probing philosophical questions like 'What is justice?', and 'What is the good?'

Plato's Intellectual Influences

Plato's philosophical career was launched by a number of things besides his own clear ability and learning. Circumstances had a role; his experience of life in Athens disposed him to respect firm and clear leadership; his regard for a hierarchical and authoritarian approach (like Sparta's) was greater than his regard for Athenian democracy; he had two relatives amongst the 'thirty tyrants', (Critias and Charmides); and he took from the already rich philosophical tradition a number of key influences.

We can note four earlier thinkers who are of importance to Plato:

- **PYTHAGORAS** - (c.550-500 BCE) had an interest in and respect for mathematics and rational thought. For Pythagoras reasoning and deduction, particularly logical and mathematical reasoning as opposed to thinking about or from experience (known as 'induction') was supreme. Religious and mystical aspects come through from Pythagoras to Plato, including the idea of the immortal soul as distinct from the transitory body.

- **PARMENIDES** - (c.480 BCE): A philosopher who developed the view that all change is provisional and so illusory, that reality, or what is 'really real', is eternal.

- **HERACLITUS** - (c.500 BCE): He argued that reality is one process of change or flux, so the one truth is that everything is dynamic and in process: the saying that 'you can't step into the same river twice', is often attributed to Heraclitus: whether he actually said this or not, it is a neat summary of his view.

- **ANAXAGORAS** - (c.500-428 BCE): He thought that reality was interconnected and that 'Mind', (nous) was what planned, structured and organised things. By 'Mind' Anaxagoras meant the rational intelligences of humans and a prior, ultimate cosmic mind to which (somehow) human minds were linked.

Plato's thinking on a wide range of issues developed over his long career, but there is a continuous theme: what is ultimately true and good is not found within the everyday visible world of what we might call 'appearance'. He thinks that if we operate with reason not the senses alone we will attain knowledge of the real and eternal. This focus on the rational or intelligible gives rise to the view that Plato has a 'two-worlds' theory where one world, the world of intellect and reason, is superior to the other, the one of sense experience. This leads to the view that Plato is a thinker who devalues the common, everyday world in favour of some kind of eternal life.

However, this is a misleading view of what Plato is doing. It is beyond doubt that Plato thinks that the human soul is immortal and that there is life of a kind both before and after death, but in his philosophy his concern is primarily with how to live well in this life. Andrew Mason writes that:

> 'Plato did not believe in a literal other world, wholly detached from this one. But he did believe that there is more in the world than we can be aware of through the senses, and that the part that is not perceptible is the most important.' (Mason 2010:2-3)

To see a little more of what Plato was about it is worth considering mathematics, which he took to exemplify rational thinking and the power of reason over the evidence we get from sense experience.

To explain why he thinks this, let's take an example:

Suppose we have the arithmetical proposition '2 + 2 =': reading it over, it is very hard to resist adding '4'. So we have '2 + 2 = 4'.

Why is that?

- **IS IT BECAUSE** you have added two and two together lots of times, and because it always comes out as four, you think it will again?

- **IS IT BECAUSE** you have had two biscuits and then two more on a number of occasions and it always amounts to four?

- **OR IS IT THAT** after learning about numbers, addition and equivalence, and doing some sums for a while, you suddenly knew that 'two plus two could not not be four'? In other words, you realised that mathematical truths are logical and rational; that whether we like it or not, two plus two can only be four.

- **SOMETHING ELSE IS CLEAR**; we can shop and buy two bottles of cola, two bottles of ginger ale, two packs of biscuits and two cartons of orange juice. We can buy two of all these things, but we can't just buy **TWO**.

Mathematical terms, concepts and relations are very significant, but they are not actual or particular in the same way as packets of biscuits or bottles of cola.

Plato nowhere discusses mathematics with these examples. But three points are clear to him:

1. Sense experience does not justify the logical truths of mathematics.

2. We cannot explain mathematics and its power as simply a product of human minds, for the truths of mathematics are not decided by us.

3. It is via intellect (not the senses) that we discover, apprehend, and can use mathematical truths.

Mathematical truths are, Plato thinks, one part of what we discover via our intellect as we apprehend the intelligible domain of forms and the 'form of the Good'.

Further to this, for Plato and his development there was a further very personal dimension that came through his acquaintance with Socrates (c. 468-399 BCE).

Plato and the influence of Socrates

Socrates is so influential that the philosophy before Socrates is termed 'Pre-Socratic 'by the historians of philosophy.

We know about Socrates through four classical writers – the historian Xenophon (c.430-355 BCE), the dramatist Aristophanes (448-380 BCE), Plato and Aristotle; all except Aristotle knew Socrates directly. Socrates came from relatively humble stock. His father was a stonemason and his mother a midwife. Plato probably remembered this when, in the Theaetetus (his dialogue concerning knowledge), he has the character 'Socrates' say that like his mother he too is a kind of midwife: he not working on the usual business of the midwife, bringing women through the physical demands of labour; he is working on the similarly challenging demeaning business of getting men to think clearly, with ideas that are 'viable and true', not 'illusory and false'.' (149a-151c)

Socrates' interest in philosophy emerged during his career in the army where he gained a reputation for his love of argument. By the time that Socrates met Plato and other young Athenians his distinctive style was well developed.

In contrast to the 'Pre-Socratic' traditions Socrates did not develop metaphysical thinking on questions about the ultimate nature of reality; the question of what amongst the flux of appearance might be constant or eternal, for example. Fire, air, spirit, earth or water were popular options amongst the Pre-Socratics.

Nor was Socrates keen on rhetoric, the art of argument for the sake of argument as promoted by the Sophists.

What Socrates was keen on, and what made him so appealing to the young Plato and to generations of philosophy students since, was his focus on ethical questions of how we should live to live well.

SUPPOSE THE FOLLOWING: In our regular lives, it is easy to see that we rely a lot on ideas of virtue such as friendship, love, courage, justice, goodness, truth and beauty. And we assume that we know what these terms mean and, perhaps, that these ideas or states will be commonly understood by others. Socrates took none of this for granted. He thought that whilst it was clear that the virtues were important to us and we habitually thought we knew what we meant by these terms, the reality was demonstrably different.

Socrates wrote nothing so far as we know. His discussions with the young intellectuals in Athens upset the authorities and he was charged with corrupting the young and with impiety towards the gods. Socrates was found guilty by the Athenian democracy and faced the death penalty. He had an opportunity to argue against this; Plato gives a presentation of this in his work Apology. He shows Socrates arguing, ironically, that if he was given a reprieve he would continue to argue and thus be an irritant to Athens, and that it would be preferable to have the peace of death, and perhaps, immortality. He does not convince the Athenians to waive the punishment, and receives the death sentence, administered via a draught of the poison hemlock. Plato is among the group of friends who accompany Socrates to prison and who witness his end. Plato finds a potent inspiration in Socrates' manner in accepting a fate that is, so far as Plato is concerned, unjust.

In the Apology Plato has Socrates say:

> 'To let no day pass without discussing goodness and all the other subjects about which you hear me talking and examining both myself and others is really the very best thing that a man can do, and that a life without this sort of examination is not worth living' (38a).

The maxim that the 'unexamined life is not worth living' is very much a Socratic challenge to all to become philosophers.

Plato and the Dialogues

Plato shaped his writing, not into the form of a technical academic treatise, in what in classical Greek philosophy was termed 'esoteric' prose, but into a distinctive 'exoteric' style, a style of writing intended to communicate to a wider audience. He did this through the innovation of writing in the form of a dialogue. Thus, Plato's works present and read rather like a play. Some dialogues are named after a character within the work, (Meno and Laches, for example) sometimes they are named after the occasion or topic at the heart of the dialogue, (Symposium and Republic, for example). At the start a scene is set and a range of characters are introduced. Invariably the characters are drawn from real life, and include friends and family of Plato as well as famous figures from Athenian life or from the history of philosophy. Perhaps they meet on a walk, or at the house of a mutual friend, they fall into conversation, and the discussion unfolds: ideas are brought up and questioned, found wanting, revised, refined and tested out against the area of life that they relate to.

Plato's second innovation is that, again as mentioned earlier, in his dialogues the character 'Socrates' appears usually as the central figure. In some of the early dialogues as well as some middle-period works, Plato writes to a degree in a biographical manner to deal with the events at the end of Socrates' life. Here Plato is paying tribute to his friend and teacher, portraying his final meetings with friends prior to his arrest, the build-up to the trial, the trial and then the time leading up to Socrates' death. Plato testifies to the inspiration Socrates provides as the person who fearlessly challenges conventions, and in Plato's writings he is, despite his fate, still a presence, and still questioning.

Whatever the topic considered in a dialogue, Socrates' technique of questioning exposes the ease with which we use terms in a fashion that is inconsistent or partial and either way limited. The outcome for those who engage in discussion with Socrates (about 'courage' for example) is that at the end, they do not then know what 'courage' is; they know what it is not, and they know that what it truly is, is important and elusive.

What Socrates was about it seems, is getting people to think for themselves and to get to an end-point in their self-understanding so that they hit a kind of barrier. One feature of the barrier that recurs is the realisation that what something really means and what it really is, is not given by any specific instance of it. This is a springboard to go on with the discussion, reviewing the ideas in question again, the better to understand them clearly. Thus empowered, the implication is that people will take greater responsibility for their thinking, and for their action. Socrates seems to think that these things are intrinsically linked. In Protagoras Plato attributes to Socrates the view that 'nobody ever willingly goes towards things that are bad for them'. It is impossible for 'human nature ... to go towards things you believe are bad for you, willingly, instead of what you think is good'. (358c-d. See also Meno 89a)

This is linked to the view that virtue is a form of knowledge, the view that if a person knows what virtue is then he would be fulfilled and happy and he would act in accordance with it. Thus to the good man no harm can come. This sits uneasily with many other traditions of thought and morality where we would argue that it is one thing to know the right thing to do and another to do it. If we choose not to do the right thing, we have chosen not to do it; for Socrates, if we know the right thing to do we will do it; if we act badly it is because we do not know the right thing in question; bad action is a consequence of ignorance; virtue is knowledge.

After Socrates's death Plato continued to discuss ideas with friends and students who came to him because of their own philosophic and intellectual interests. It seems that putting together a dialogue to reflect the state or stage of thinking he had reached became a regular activity. Eventually Plato was able to write in such a fashion as to make allusions to earlier dialogues and we can infer from this that he is working with reference to a readership familiar with the ideas he refers to.

Over time there is a shift in the role that Plato gives to Socrates in the dialogues. Socrates is always present (except in the late dialogue, Laws), usually as the key figure in each dialogue. The early period writings focus on ethical issues that are Socratic in character, but as Plato matures he develops his own interests and agenda. 'Socrates' the character becomes a means by which he explores his concerns. The other characters are also varying expressions of Plato's mind at work. This is evident as Plato reaches his so-called 'middle period'. In works such as Republic and Phaedrus a wider range of philosophical and political problems are reviewed and positive 'Platonic' theories are explored. The 'late period' includes works such as Parmenides, Theaetetus, Sophist, Statesman, and Laws, and these writings involve a re-assessment, criticism and refinement of many of the ideas set out in the middle period works.

A common feature of Plato's work is that for a given problem a variety of views or definitions are tried out and found wanting. We are left with a better understanding of the problem, but not necessarily given a solution; a method of questioning and the cultivation of a more critical outlook, rather than the provision of a solution to the problems that have been reviewed. The Platonic technique here seems to be, 'Well, here are the options, what do you want to buy into – and how will you justify it?'

A relevant example is that in some dialogues, the Phaedo and the Republic for example, Plato sets out variants of the so-called **THEORY OF FORMS**.

Here we come to a major point:

Plato **NEVER** devotes a specific work to giving a **DEFINITIVE** account of the 'theory of Forms'.

Although many take this theory as the core doctrine of 'what Platonism is', it is more an evolving theory referred to in several dialogues, often with the impression being that is the ideas have been in discussion outside the dialogue in question. Sometimes it is linked to beauty (Symposium); at other times the good (or the form of the Good) is discussed (in Meno and Republic, for example). Yet in the Parmenides the theory of Forms is, via the character Parmenides, subjected to a severe critique; the theory is not abandoned, but it is given a distinct overhaul and strong lines of criticism are presented. Overall the key feature is Plato's philosophic technique of ongoing critical debate which predominates over the safety of buying wholesale into a theory.

There is another aspect to Plato's use of dialogues and to his habit of leaving questions and debates open for ongoing discussion. It is that as a philosopher and as a teacher, Plato thought that the most effective way to get to the truest understanding of an issue was through discussion within an academic community.

In Phaedrus (275-276) he has Socrates explain that writing is fixed and one-dimensional. Texts in any case can only circulate amongst those who understand them, and a text can't choose its readers. There is a much better way, which is when a person with 'real knowledge of right and beauty and good' engages in discussion with others. In his Seventh Letter, Plato similarly explains that the issues he is interested in can best be grasped by 'long partnership in a common life', by a process of active discussion 'in which questions and answers are exchanged in good faith and without malice', thereby 'human capacity is stretched to its limit' and understanding and intelligence 'illuminates the subjects' under review (341, 344). Written work is, he suggests, inadequate for the expression of our best and most serious ideas.

Plato's reservation is that the written word will not engage and provoke discussion. Despite these reservations, Plato wants to write, and it makes perfect sense for him to adapt the dramatic literary form of a play into the philosophical dialogue, where a discussion can be presented and where, as we have explained, the debate can be left open for ongoing refinement. The further benefit is that Plato the thinker can hide himself behind the text of the dialogue: it is to be noted that Plato never appears as a participant within a dialogue, but of course he writes each one as a whole to explore problems of his choosing.

The development and use of dialogue form is one of Plato's greatest achievements.

The Theory of Forms: The Good and Bees

As we noted earlier, the theories of definitive importance that the OCR specification sets centre on the 'theory of Forms', especially the 'form of the Good', and on the importance to expressing them of the 'analogy of the Cave'. We can also re-state that the OCR specification wants candidates to 'understand what Plato meant' by his notion of 'Forms' and be able to demonstrate knowledge and understanding of 'the relation between concepts and phenomena', and the concept of 'Ideals'.

As a way into looking at these matters, let's begin with a hypothetical reflection.

Suppose it is the end of the day. Imagine that you think back and say, 'It's been a **GOOD** day.' The weather has been bright and sunny; it was good weather. You enjoyed a good breakfast and the commute to work was easy, so that was good too. Work went well. A report you'd written good feedback. You met a good friend at lunch and were able to catch up and, well that was good. In the evening there was time to read more of **SUTREE**, by Cormack McCarthy, such a good book. When preparing supper you'd listened to some of Mozart's **DON GIOVANNI** (really good music) and then the late film was the last of the Millennium trilogy, **THE GIRL WHO KICKED THE HORNET'S NEST**. You'd missed it when it had last been shown, so it was good to watch it now.

Thinking it over, it had been a **GOOD** day, and all through there had been a lot of different **GOODS**.

You may not have had a day exactly like the one you have just imagined, but it is not so unlikely that you have used the word 'good' in a wide range of ways. You might have had occasion to talk about having a **GOOD TIME**, a **GOOD DEAL**, a **GOOD PEN**, and **GOOD NIGHT'S SLEEP**, a **GOOD HOLIDAY**, a **GOOD REVISION SESSION** or a **GOOD CUP OF COFFEE**. Now here we have, with the time, deal, pen, night's sleep, holiday, revision session and coffee, seven particular instances of one concept, 'good', or 'goodness'.

Here we have examples of what Plato would consider the relationship to be **BETWEEN CONCEPTS AND PHENOMENA**.

Suppose you consider that a good book is not the same as a good deal, and that neither are the same as a good holiday or a good friend. We could go on, but hopefully the point is clear: all these various things, states or relations are describable as 'good', yet all are distinct. None of them is the sum total of what 'goodness' is.

The core question arises: **IN VIRTUE OF WHAT ARE THEY ALL 'GOOD'**? How is it that we can equally well use the same term in relation to so many different cases?

One solution would be to say that 'good' signals an individual's positive approval of the things, state or relation in question. So a day, a commute, a holiday, a book, a friend, a film, a meal and so on, are 'good' if, and only if, the person whose day, commute, holiday, book, friend, film and/or meal it was, approves of it.

Another solution would be to say that for all of the things, states and relations in question there are specific criteria for a good, as opposed to a poor or indifferent day, commute, holiday, book, friend, film and/or meal.

The **FIRST** view would give a version of **SUBJECTIVISM**; the **SECOND** view gives a type of **RELATIVISM**.

There may be good reasons to defend subjectivism and/or relativism, but with regard to the issue of 'the good' one definite thing that can be said about Plato is that he disagrees strongly with both relativism and subjectivism. He is much more supportive of the view that 'goodness itself' is an **IDEAL** that has a reality over and above the particular and limited 'goods'.

Let's take these issues further via an exploration of some ideas in Plato's Meno.

The dialogue starts with a question Meno asks Socrates:

> '… is being good something you can be taught?' (70a)

Meno offers alternatives: perhaps being good is learnt by practice? Perhaps it comes naturally? Socrates says he has no idea what the good is. The question returns to Meno. What does he think 'being good is'? (70d).

Meno gives examples of how people at different ages or stages life can be good, and he concludes that being good 'is… different for each of us; it varies according to what we are doing, according to how old we are, and according to our role in life.' (72a). Meno has in effect proposed a form of moral relativism; 'the good' is relative to the age, condition and interests of each person.

Socrates congratulates Meno on the 'swarm' of suggestions he has made, but then takes up the image of the swarm and switches from the good to bees: suppose he had asked about bees instead, what would Meno have said? Socrates suggests that, analogous to his reply on the question of the good, Meno would have said that bees were many and varied. We now know there are around 25,000 types of bee, and Plato doubtless knew that there were many types of bee.

Socrates advances to a key question:

> '... what's the respect in which there's no difference from bee to bee? What is it that makes them all the same thing?' (72c)

Socrates gets Meno's agreement that he could come up with an answer to this question, but rather than get it Socrates moves back to the question of what the good is:

> '... do the same with cases of being good. Even if there are a lot of them, and lots of different sorts, they must at least have some single form, something that makes them all cases of being good.' (72c)

Here in the Meno, with the help of some bees, Plato gives us one of his earlier examples of 'theory of Forms.'

Whether we consider bees, or cases of being good, Plato thinks that what in essence makes a bee a bee or a good action 'good', is **NOT** what is given in the example in question. **NO ONE BEE** can tell us **ALL** that any bee can be, and **NO ONE CASE** of **BEING GOOD** definitively exhausts what **THE GOOD** is.

When Plato asks, via Socrates, what the case of different examples of being good have in common to make them all cases of being good, he uses the phrase '**SOME SINGLE FORM**'. In the **REPUBLIC** (472c) when he is discussing what justice is **IN ITSELF**, Plato refers to the 'ideal pattern', suggesting that the 'form of justice' is analogous to a kind of template. In cases of goodness, Plato is in effect **CONTRASTING PARTICULAR EXAMPLES** with **THE IDEAL** or **UNIVERSAL** concept (goodness-itself), and his longer-term suggestion is that **THE GOOD-ITSELF**, or **THE 'FORM OF THE GOOD'**, is the ideal goodness-itself, abstract but objectively real and true, independent of and prior to all particular cases. An implication of this view is that the reality of **PARTICULAR** cases, of bees, goodness and GCE examinations, is **DISTINCT FROM** and **SUBORDINATE TO** the objective and really real domain of forms.

In light of this, we can reflect on the following definition of the theory of Forms:

> 'The essential feature of this theory is that reality is only to be found in a world of eternal and unchanging Forms, of which the shifting phenomena of the sensible world are imperfect imitations or copies, and to which the latter owe such half-reality as they possess. The Forms are in fact universals given the status of independent and absolute entities... The Forms, arranged in a hierarchy at the head of which stands the Form of the Good, constitute the only true objects of knowledge...' (W Hamilton in Plato, 1973:17).

It is worth looking back over the discussion of 'bees and the good' to see how many aspects of this definition can be found.

The Theory of Forms: Arguments from Opposites and from Equality

Another line of thinking Plato develops on the theory forms can be traced via the 'argument from opposites' found in the **PHAEDO** and the 'argument from equality' that we also find in the **REPUBLIC**.

The **ARGUMENT FROM OPPOSITES** works from the view that in general opposites imply each other. Various examples are given: beauty and ugliness, large and small, right and wrong, fast and slow, just and unjust, sleeping and waking, and life and death.

Next, it is argued that these opposites involve a 'process of generation from each to other'. (Phaedo 71a)

To take one example: A person is awake, but eventually they sleep. After sleeping they wake, till in due time they sleep again, and so it goes on. As this is in general true the idea is that we have every reason to see life and death similarly. Thus death will generate life, and life death, and so on. The argument is then if this were not so, and if 'generation were a straight path to the opposite extreme' (72b), then eventually everything would reach the same end state and 'change would cease altogether'. Against this, Plato assumes the much greater coherence of the cyclical view of the processes of reality that was common to Greek thought at this time, and he thinks he has shown that the soul (as distinct from the body) is immortal.

Plato also uses the 'argument from opposites' to lay out a view about the theory of Forms. He thinks that we could say that the faster comes from the slower, and the slower from the faster.

Consider this example:

Imagine eight athletes lining up for a 100 metre sprint. They are stationary on their blocks; when the starting pistol detonates the athletes move forward. With each stride they accelerate, so each is moving faster than the stride before. That previous stride was slower: after about thirty metres all of the athletes are running as fast as they can, some are a bit faster than others, who are slower, and the one who sustains his pace as the fastest to the finishing line wins. As the athletes pass the finishing line they slow and come to a stop.

In this case, and in any other using other pair of opposites, the contrasts between fast and slow, beautiful and ugly, heavy and light and so on is something we notice. But nothing, we should also see, is fast or heavy or beautiful as such. We make judgments about how fast, heavy or beautiful particular things might be, by appeal to an abstract standard distinct from any actual occurrence.

Plato takes this point up later in Phaedo with the famous discussion of equality. (73d)

We are asked to imagine considering two sticks to be equal length, or two stones to be of equal weight. Here are judgements are made with reference that which is 'distinct from' and 'beyond' the sticks and stones in question, namely 'absolute equality'. Sticks and stones, and many other things, of course, can be variously equal in dimension, weight, colour and so on, but in no case is 'absolute equality' manifest. In this version of the 'theory of Forms', Plato develops the following explanation of equality, and such notions as Beauty and Goodness: they are 'patterns' of which we judge the 'copies'.

NOTE THAT HERE the forms are defined as patterns, and the ideas of absolute Beauty and Goodness are said to exist 'in the fullest possible sense'. (Phaedo, 77b)

PLATO REVISITS THIS DISCUSSION in Republic (523a-524d).

Socrates explaining how some perceptions require to our use of thought because perception alone cannot give 'a trustworthy result.' Sensations where what we experience is uniform will not need further thought. However, where our perceptions are of contraries and are ambiguous, thought will needed. This time the examples used are the middle, third and little fingers three fingers of ones' hand. Look at any one of them and at each in turn and there is no question arising; each is a finger. If we then look at them all we see that the middle finger is the longest and largest; the little finger is shortest and smallest; the third finger is longer than the little finger and shorter than the middle finger, so it is both longer and smaller. If we relied on the sense of touch alone, we would have similar difficulties with thickness, thinness, hardness and softness; objects can be perceived as having contrary qualities or attributes and finding the truth would be very difficult by the senses alone.

But Plato thinks that by thought we can reason that the definitional questions about longer, shorter and so on can be pursued, on the basis of the distinctions between the intelligible and the visible. Plato thinks that reason can grasp the intelligible truths of the abstract forms distinct from how things appear in the visible realm.

Plato's Theory of Forms, the Form of the Good and the Analogy of the Cave

Plato wrote **REPUBLIC** in c.375 BCE. Plato's aims included a study of the ways a state might be governed so as to develop a better theory of justice. Plato argues that an ideal just society requires governance by the wisest ruler. The wisest ruler cannot be one of the common run of citizens who make up the Athenian democracy. The wisest ruler will be one who has had a philosophical training of an advanced kind, who learns how to differentiate between opinion, belief and knowledge. Philosophers will learn to know the forms, the form of justice, and ultimately, the form of the Good. Therefore they, but particularly, the best of them, will be able to rule justly. The philosopher-ruler is proposed as the just ruler. **REPUBLIC** then sets out a programme of study for the philosopher-ruler. Plato has a strong visual imagination and he constructs what modern thinkers would term 'thought experiments' to illustrate his theories. In **REPUBLIC** he gives three successive images: **THE SIMILIE OF THE SUN**, **THE DIVIDED LINE** and then **THE SIMILIE** (or Analogy) **OF THE CAVE**. It is the last of these that the OCR examination has focus on, but given that Plato writes the sequence of the three similes, and that he did so originally for his own students to work through, it seems wise to look at each in turn.

THE SIMILE OF THE SUN

In Book VI of the **REPUBLIC** Plato is developing a scheme for the education of philosopher-rulers. The question arises, is there a higher form of knowledge than justice? Socrates says that the 'highest form of knowledge is knowledge of the form of the good, from which things that are just and so on derive their usefulness and value.' (505a)

A handy definition to note - and there are more useful points to come.

There follows a discussion as to whether the good is to be defined as a type of pleasure or as a type of knowledge. Socrates avoids these alternatives: the good is 'the end of all endeavour, the object on which every heart is set, whose existence it divines'. (505d)

The form of the good, says Socrates, is very hard to grasp; he is pressed to give fuller explanation. He says that such a task is beyond him, but he will tell of something that seems to be a 'child of the good'.

This turns out to be **THE SIMILE OF THE SUN**.

Socrates says there are many particular things that we think good, or beautiful and so on, but this leads on to the suggestion that there is 'beauty-itself' and 'good-itself' and the like for each set or class of things, and from this we 'posit by contrast a single form, which is unique, in each case, and call it "what really is" each thing.' (507b)

Socrates confirms that particulars are objects of sight not intelligence, and that the forms are objects of **INTELLECT** not **SIGHT**. He gives examples from various senses to suggest that there is something significant about sight.

AN EXAMPLE WILL HELP - Suppose four people are standing around in a sculpture park and they all agree that the piece of work they are looking at is beautiful. Plato's point is that for the four people to register the beauty of the sculpture an additional element is needed, and that is light, and light, in our open-air example especially chosen, comes from the sun. The sun is not identical with sight not with the object seen, but the sun enables sight, and in a way it infuses the eye with the capacity to see (508a-b).

Socrates then makes the simile with the good: the sun is 'the child of the good';

'The good has begotten its own likeness, and it bears the same

relation to sight and visible objects in the visible realm as the good bears to intelligence and intelligible objects in the intelligible realm.' (508c)

Just as we see less well at dusk or at night, so our power to know the truth and to know the good is diminished if the mind is fixed on the 'twilight world of change and decay', but when the 'mind's eye is fixed on objects illuminated by truth and reality, it understands and knows them, and its possession of intelligence is evident'. (508d-e)

Just as the sun is the enabler of sight and the source of the warmth that generates growth, so the good 'may be said to the source not only of the intelligibility of the objects of knowledge, but also of their being and reality; yet it is not itself that reality, but is beyond it, and superior to it in dignity and power.' (509b)

Notice how 'the good' is the 'source' of the 'being and reality' and the 'intelligibility' of the particulars.

THE SIMILIE OF THE SUN in summary form:

THE VIABLE WORLD	THE INTELLIGIBLE WORLD
The Sun	The Good
The source of warmth, growth and light, which makes objects of sense visible and empowers the faculty of sight	The source of being and truth, which gives intelligibility to the forms and objects of thought, and rational capacity to the mind

THE DIVIDED LINE

Here Plato (See Republic 510a-511e) has Socrates give instructions to draw out a line, divided into two unequal parts, with each part divided again in the same ratio. Plato imagines his line being drawn vertically, but to explain and illustrate what he means we will be working with a horizontal diagram.

In the diagram below line A is the initial line to be drawn:

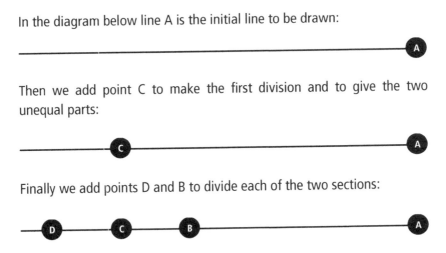

Then we add point C to make the first division and to give the two unequal parts:

Finally we add points D and B to divide each of the two sections:

Thus we have four zones; A, B, C, and D, but Plato wants us to imagine an ascending movement from section D to section A of the line. As we are using a horizontal line, we need to think more of a sliding scale from left to right giving zone D, then zones D-C, C-B and B-A.

Socrates then explains how the various parts of the line so divided can be used to bracket off the following, listed here in no particular order:

- the world of appearance

- mathematical reasoning

- the intelligible world

- forms

- belief (pistis)

- mathematical objects

- illusion (eikasia)

- knowledge (episteme)

- the form of the good

- visible things

- intelligence (noesis)

- opinion (doxa)

It is a good idea to draw a large scale version of what is to follow.

SECTIONS D-C REPRESENTS THE 'WORLD OF APPEARANCE'	SECTIONS B-A REPRESENTS THE 'INTELLIGIBLE WORLD'
Here illusion or belief gives rise to opinion.	Here reasoning and intelligence lead to knowledge.
Below section D-C are what we access via illusion and belief: Images/shadows and visible objects.	Below section A-C are the objects of knowledge accessed via reason and intelligence: Mathematical Objects, Forms/the Form of the Good.

So:

The "world of appearance"
Opinion

The "intelligible" world
Knowledge

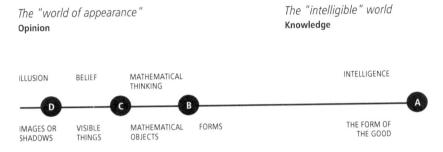

Unpicking The Divided Line

For Plato the human condition means that in a sense we inhabit two domains: there is the domain of appearance, of visible things, and the domain of intelligible things.

The visible domain is what surrounds us: what we experience via our senses; this visible world is a world of change and uncertainty. This Plato's reworking of the world of flux as proposed by Heraclitus.

The intelligible domain is made up of the understanding of concepts and ideas grasped through reason: anything arising through intellectual activity, such as abstract definitions or mathematics, makes up this intelligible world, which is the 'really real' world of objective reality. This is a re-jig of the one eternal reality of Parmenides.

Plato's theory is a development of both Heraclitus and Parmenides into one coherent theory, or so Plato hopes. As the diagram of the divided line shows, the intelligible domain contains the eternal 'Forms'; the visible domain is, in some way, the imperfect and changing manifestation of this world of unchanging forms which are the true source of being, meaning and value.

For example, the 'Form' of a horse is intelligible, abstract, and applies to all horses; even though horses vary among themselves, the 'form of the Horse' would never change even if every horse in the world were to vanish. An individual horse is a physical, changing object that can easily (via sudden death) cease to be a horse, but the 'form of the Horse', or 'horsiness-itself' never changes. Plato's view would be that as an individual physical object, a specific horse only makes sense in that it can be referred to the 'form' of 'horsiness'.

As we mentioned earlier, a common conclusion to reach when thinking about the visible and intelligible worlds is that Plato is offering a 'two-worlds' theory. Later Christian interpretations of Plato favour this view. But is does not seem that Plato intends this. Myles Burnyeat argues that 'one should be careful about using phrases like "the world of Forms" or "another world". Plato uses them but the contrast he has in mind is not, as one might have thought, a contrast between one set of particular things and then another set completely like it except more perfect, more abstract, and located somewhere else, in some heaven somewhere.'

Burnyeat offers this explanation of Plato's purpose:

> 'His contrast is between the particular and the general. Those questions, "What is justice?, "What is beauty?", etc., are general questions , questions about justice and beauty in general. They are not question about the here and the now… If you are asking "What is beauty?, you are not asking "Who is the most beautiful person in this room?" And if you are not thinking about the here and now, then, in the sense Plato is interested in, you are not here and now. You are where your mind is, not because you are in some other particular place but a

better one, but because you are not in place in that sense at all. You are immersed in generalities. So it is all right to use the phrase, "the world of Forms", provided one understands it to mean the realm of invariable generalities.' (Burnyeat in Magee 1987:23)

Returning to the 'Divided Line', Plato thus imagines representing these two perspectives on reality, the visible or sensible, and the intelligible, as existing on a line that can be divided: one section of the line, C-A on the diagram, represents the intelligible world and the sections covered by D and C make up the visible world.

Each part of the line also relates to a certain type of understanding: of the visible world, we have at worst, mere opinion and at best belief; of the intelligible world via reasoning we achieve knowledge. Each of these divisions on the line can also be divided. Thus the visible world can be divided into a qualitatively lower region, 'illusion', which is Plato thinks is made up of shadows, reflections, paintings, poetry, and so on, and an qualitatively higher region, 'belief,' which refers to any kind of knowledge of physical objects, the things that change, such as individual horses. 'Belief' may be true some or most of the time but occasionally is wrong (since things in the visible world change); belief is practical and may serve as a relatively reliable guide to life but it doesn't really involve thinking things out to the point of certainty.

The intelligible world (A-C on the diagram) can be divided into reasoning as in mathematics, which is knowledge of the concepts and rules of mathematics which require that some postulates be accepted without question, and then as we move to knowledge of forms we employ 'intelligence,' and so achieve knowledge of the highest and most abstract categories of things, and understanding of the ultimate 'Form of the Good'.

We can thus see that with the Divided Line, Plato gives a concept map of the ideas sketched in the Simile of the Sun. Just as the Good, analogous to the Sun's provision of light, gives being and truth to all, so in the Divided Line, the Form of the Good is what validates and informs all the forms (of courage, beauty, truth, and so on). And these pure objects of knowledge are apprehended and known via reason and intellect. If we do not use our minds, Plato implies, we will be locked into the visible world of change, and we risk sinking into illusion.

To explore things further Plato moves to his most famous literary analogy, the Analogy of the Cave.

THE ANALOGY OF THE CAVE

The analogy of the Cave is set out in the Republic VII (514a-517c). Plato calls the narrative a 'picture' and later a 'simile' (see 514a and 517b), and it has been termed an allegory as well as an analogy. As we have said, it is what in modern philosophy we'd call a 'thought experiment', a kind of parabolic story that is a fiction used to portray issues of importance. It is perhaps best to leave for a moment what we call this narrative and just read it. Since the text is not set for study by OCR a usual approach would be to have a summary of it to discuss and analyse, but here we have the 'stretch and challenge' of studying the text. Over the next few pages the main part of the text of analogy is set out. The standard line numbers have been inserted to aid the commentary notes which come at the end. It is a good idea to read the extract at least twice before moving on.

Socrates is in conversation with Glaucon

(514a) 'I want you to go on to picture the enlightenment or ignorance of our human condition somewhat as follows. Imagine an underground chamber like a cave, which has a long entrance open to the daylight and as wide as the cave. In this chamber are men who have been prisoners there since they were children, their legs and necks being so fastened that they can only look straight ahead of them and cannot turn their heads. (514b) Some way off behind and higher up, a fire is burning, and between the fire and the prisoners and above them runs a road, in front of which a curtain-wall has been built, like a screen at puppet shows between the operators and their audience, above which they show their puppets.'

'I see.'

(514c) 'Imagine further that there are men carrying all sorts of gear along behind the curtain-wall, projecting above it and including figures of men and animals made of wood and stone and all sorts of other materials, and that some of these men, as you would expect, are talking, and some are not.'   (515a)

'An odd picture and an odd sort of prisoner.'

'They are drawn from life,' I replied. 'For, tell me, do you think our prisoners could see anything of themselves or their fellows

except the shadows thrown by the fire on the wall of the cave opposite them?'

'How could they see anything else if they were prevented from moving their heads all their lives?'

'And would they see anything more of the objects carried along the road?' (515b)

'Of course not.'

'Then if they were able to talk to each other, would they not assume that the shadows they saw were the real things?'

'Inevitably.'

'And if the wall of their prison opposite them reflected sound, don't you think they would suppose, whenever one of the passers-by on the road spoke, that the voice belonged to the shadow passing before them?'

'They would be bound to think so.'

And so in every way they would believe that the shadows of the objects we mentioned were the whole truth.' (515c)

'Yes, inevitably.'

'Then think what would naturally happen to them if they were are released from their bonds and cured of their delusions. Suppose on of them were let loose, and suddenly compelled to stand up and turn his head and look and walk towards the fire; (515d) all these action would be painful and he would be too dazzled to see properly the objects of which he used to see the shadows. What do you think he would say if he was told that what he used to see was so much empty nonsense and that he was now nearer reality and seeing more correctly, because he was turned towards objects that were more real, and on top of that he was compelled to say what each of the passing objects was when it was pointed out to him? Don't you think he would be at a loss, and think that what he used to see was far truer than the things being shown to him?'

'Yes, far truer.'

(515e) 'And if he were made to look directly at the light of the fire, it would hurt his eyes and he would turn back and retreat to the things which he could see properly, which he would think really clear than the things being shown to him.'

'Yes.'

'And if... he were forcibly dragged up the steep and rugged ascent and not let go until he had been dragged out into the sunlight, (516a) the process would be a painful one, to which he would much object, and when he merged into the light his eyes would be so dazzled by the glare of it that he wouldn't be able to see a single one of the things he was now told were real.'

Certainly not at first, he agreed.'

'Because, of course, he would need to grow accustomed to the light before he could se things in the upper world outside the cave. First he will find it easiest to look at the shadows, next the reflections of men and other objects in water, and later on at the objects themselves. After that he would find it easier to observe the heavenly bodies and the sky itself at night, (516b) and to look at the light of the moon and the stars rather than at the sun and its light by day.'

Of course.

'The thing he would b able to do at last would be to look directly at the sun itself and gaze at it without using reflections on water or any other medium, but as it is in itself.'

'That must come last.'

'Later on he would come to the conclusion that it is the sun that produces the changing seasons and years and controls everything in the visible world, and is in a sense responsible for *everything that he and his fellow prisoners used to see.' (516c)*

'That is the conclusion he would obviously reach.'

And when he thought of his first home and what passed for wisdom there, and of his fellow prisoners, don't you think he would congratulate himself on his good fortune and be sorry to for them?'

'Very much so.'

'There was probably a certain amount of honour and glory to won among the prisoners, and prizes for keen sightedness for those best able to remember the order of sequence among the passing shadows and so be best able to divine their future appearances. (516d) Will our released prisoner hanker after those prizes or envy this power and honour? Won't he be more likely to feel, as Homer says, that he would far rather be "a serf in the house of some landless man", or indeed, anything else in the world, that hold the opinions and live the life that they do?'

'Yes', he replied, 'he would prefer anything to a life like theirs.' (516e)

'Then what do you think would happen... if he went back to sit in his old seat in the cave? Wouldn't his eyes be blinded by the darkness, because he had come in so suddenly out of the

sunlight?

'Certainly.'

And if he had to discriminate between the shadows, in competition with the other prisoners, (517a) while he was still blinded and before his eyes got used to the darkness - a process that would take some time - wouldn't he be likely to make a fool of himself? And they would say that his visit to the upper world had ruined his sight, and the ascent was not worth even attempting. And if anyone tried to release them and lead them up, they would kill him if they could lay hands on him.'

'They certainly would.'

Plato then has Socrates explain the analogy

'Now my dear Glaucon… this simile must be connected throughout with what preceded it. (517b) The realm revealed by sight corresponds to the prison, and the light of the fire in the prison to the power of the sun. And you won't go wrong if you if you connect the ascent into the upper world and the sight of the objects there with the upward progress of the mind into the intelligible region. That at any rate is my interpretation, which is what you are anxious to hear; the truth of the matter is, after all, known only to god. But in my opinion, for what it is worth, the

final thing to be perceived in the intelligible region, and perceived only with difficulty, (517c) is the form of good; once seen it is inferred to be responsible for whatever is right and valuable in anything, producing in the visible region light and the source of light, and being in the intelligible region itself controlling source of truth and intelligence. And anyone who is going to act rationally either in public or in private must have sight of it.'

Commentary on the Analogy of the Cave

We have not quite reached the end of the narrative of the Cave, but before we discuss the final section it is worth re-reading the sections above and then considering some points of commentary which are made with reference to the standard line numbers.

1. 514a 'picture'; 517b 'simile': As mentioned earlier, the narrative works as a 'thought experiment' to illustrate in a particular way the issues that are under discussion. As the narrative is extended and has a range of components it is a very extensive 'picture' or 'simile'; reading it through we may well think it is more a 'picture' analogous to a film, and that the similitudes or comparisons are extensive and connected in ways that are also analogous. All in all it makes good sense to consider the narrative as a sequence of analogies.

2. 514a onwards: In general with the whole narrative it is important to master the details. For example, the prisoners are fastened by 'neck' and 'legs': we are not told how they are

fastened or what they are fastened with. It is unwise to make anything up to fill the gaps. However, we are told that they have been fastened since they were children. In what way might that be significant to Plato? Look at the opening line: the 'picture' is showing the 'enlightenment or ignorance' of 'our human condition'. Here is another point many miss: Plato makes it clear, the focus is on OUR enlightenment or ignorance. Plato is raising a generic question about the human condition; the state of the prisoners at the start of the narrative is one way of being; the condition of the prisoner who is released and who eventually makes it into the daylight to see the sun 'as it is', is another. Plato is suggesting that we all face the same options.

3. 514b-c: The scenario that is depicted is all for the sake of certain effects; what do we think of how the prisoners are situated? It is odd, unusual, or wrong? Is it, Plato wants us to think, natural? Is it how things should be? What about the various aspects of the interior of the Cave; so far as the prisoners are concerned, they add up to a compelling reality, but we as readers, outside the narrative, know it is a world of shadow and sound, a world of appearances separated from reality, and separated by the constraints that the prisoners unknowingly have.

4. 515b: We can see here that Plato makes it clear that the prisoners are making valid assumptions from the evidence that they have. They are reasoning from partial sensory awareness, and are (515c) in a state of true belief. This is a form of knowledge that Plato goes on to review in detail in his dialogue Theaetetus (201a-c). There we have Socrates explaining that a skilled lawyer can convince a jury that something they have not directly experienced is, for all that, true. Of course, it is the job of the lawyer to convince the jury, but if he succeeds, whilst it is

true that the jury may have beliefs they think are true, it is obvious that this cannot be genuine knowledge: knowledge cannot logically be the same as the beliefs we think true. Back in the Cave, the prisoners have 'true belief', relative to the very obvious constraints they operate under, but they don't, when they are fastened, have real knowledge. Plato reinforces this in Theaetetus: 'knowledge is not located in immediate experiences, but in reasoning about it, since the latter apparently, but not the former, makes it possible to grasp being and truth.' (186d) Later in Republic (523a-524d) we come the argument that whilst it is natural that rely on our everyday perceptions for much of time, we find that 'contrary perceptions' require the use of reflection and thought. This is developed by the example we considered earlier, when Socrates considers the middle, third and little fingers on a person's hand and shows that as soon as we ask about the relative size of the fingers we have the contrary perception of the third finger being larger than the little finger and smaller than the middle finger. It is via reason that we can consider 'larger' and 'smaller' as distinct qualities and of course, we do this by operating in the intelligible as opposed to the visible domain.

5. 515c-d: Here it worth looking at how the narrative works; we are reminded we are in an illustration and we have to re-imagine a sequence of 'what ifs' or 'suppose that's'. Now we have to 'suppose that' the prisoners are 'released from their bonds and cured of their delusions.' Again we see Plato's preference for knowledge via reasoning rather than from subjective sense experience. Relying on shadow and sound is analogous to relying on partial sense experience, and this is a state of 'delusion', which is taking the illusion of the Divided Line to a greater extreme. In fact, the prisoners collectively are not released, but

we asked to imagine what would happen if one was 'let loose'; he'd be 'compelled to stand up and turn his head.' Think about this from within the analogy. How difficult would it be to stand? How natural would it seem? How painful and frightening would it be? And turning one's head, using the neck muscles for the first time? It is going to hurt a lot and be very scary for the prisoner who has, in all probability, no recollection of what he did as a child (if you remember the opening line?) All the challenge and fear that might be imagined here is relayed through Plato's reference to compulsion; the prisoner would not choose to do any of the things open to him once he is released; he had to be forced to something that, with some understatement, Plato says is 'painful'.

6. 515d-e: Note how Plato puts emphasis on how the initial experiences of the released prisoner will be confusing and counter-intuitive. Stress is laid on how hard it will be for the prisoner to overcome his former view of what was true. Again we need to keep the opening of the narrative before us: how far is 'our human condition enlightened or ignorant'? The prisoner is exemplifying the pain and difficulty anyone would experience when we try to make the transition towards philosophical insight from everyday belief within the world of appearance, from the shadow world of delusion within the Cave, towards the enlightenment of knowledge of the intelligible domain, the daylight and the sun in the narrative. So great is the difficulty that it is more attractive for the prisoner to retreat back to his place in the Cave; similarly many will shy away from the quest for philosophical knowledge.

7. 515e-516a: Through this section it is again helpful to remember this is a fictional thought experiment and that if we imagine

telling this story we would surely lace this section with dramatic humour; it is not a literal description of a recommended style of teaching! The prisoner is 'forcibly dragged' out of the Cave and up the rugged path and into the daylight. This, together with the objections the prisoner makes, press home the impression of the difficulties that come with the philosophical journey from ignorance to enlightenment; Plato is never shy of making the point that philosophy is hard!

8. 516a-e: Here we have a series of steps in the transition phase outside the Cave. By degrees the prisoner becomes accustomed to operating in the outside world, via shadows (playing another role here), reflections in water, and the night sky; eventually he is able to look 'directly at the sun itself', and then he will see it 'as it is itself.' He will see that it 'controls everything' and is 'responsible for everything' in the visible world. One must issue a health and safety warning and say that this looking at the sun direct business is not something to try at home! However, within the analogy of the Cave this is Plato's key line and we can see the link to the Simile of the Sun and to the Divided Line: again, the sun as it is in itself is a simile for the form of the Good, and the prisoner's ascent from the Cave to the full daylight when he can contemplate the sun direct is a dramatised progress along the Divided Line, from illusion to intelligence. Possessed of wisdom, the prisoner now feels sorry for his fellows still trapped in the Cave. But he will congratulate himself on his 'good fortune'. He will no longer hanker after the prizes that arose from the competitions in the Cave.

9. 516e-517a: Here is a reversed transition as we are asked to consider 'what would happen if' the prisoner was to return to Cave. If he was to return to take up his seat alongside his former

associates he would be blinded by the dark, so he would no longer be able to compete well in the shadow world; he would face scorn and ridicule; the view would arise that his trip had been pointless, and those who remained in the Cave, the majority of course, would consider the journey out a complete waste of time. Here Plato makes a strong teaching point about the perils of philosophical work: that the challenge of getting people to think for themselves can be a thankless one. And there is added edge, it is commonly thought, when the narrative moves on to say that so sure of their own position are they, that the other prisoners would, if they could, kill anyone who tried to release them: this is thought to be an indirect reference back to the historical fate of Socrates. Note that Plato does not actually write that the prisoners would kill the released prisoner: it is 'anyone' who would try to release them.

10. 517b-c: Plato has Socrates provide Glaucon with a pretty clear explanation of the 'simile', as it is called here. All of the points are important:

'…this simile must be connected throughout with what preceded it.'

Plato surely means the ideas developed in the pervious parts of the dialogue, the Simile of the Sun and the Divided Line.

We then have a list of points of comparison:

1. 'The realm revealed by sight corresponds to the prison'

2. 'The light of the fire in the prison (corresponds) to the power of the sun.'

3. 'The ascent into the upper world and the sight of the objects there (corresponds) with the upward progress of the mind into the intelligible region.'

4. 'The final thing to be perceived in the intelligible region, and perceived only with difficulty, is the form of good; once seen it is inferred to be responsible for whatever is right and valuable in anything, producing in the visible region light and the source of light, and being in the intelligible region itself controlling source of truth and intelligence.'

Within this Socrates is given line of qualification: he says that the explanation is 'at any rate is my interpretation, which is what you are anxious to hear; the truth of the matter is, after all, known only to god.'

This is very typical of Plato. Contrary to the view that he is doctrinaire thinker with very definite, fixed theories, he is much more an experimentalist, one who presents ideas always with an opportunity for them to be challenged, developed, or criticised. Here he seems to have Socrates set out a view of a particular theory, and then in a throwaway line say something like, 'Well, this is maybe how it is, but who knows? And what do you think?' This is Plato the educator at work, always encouraging his students and readers to think for themselves.

▸ The Final Section of the Cave Narrative (517c-521b)

In the final stage of the discussion Socrates expresses a point often overlooked. From the simile confusion from being unsighted comes in one of two ways; by being dazzled by unaccustomed brightness or blinded by unexpected darkness, analogous to the prisoner being released and undergoing the transition towards the light, and his subsequent return to the blinding darkness when he goes back to his seat. Plato has Socrates challenge the elitist view that the philosopher who has rational insight and has, in the world of the analogy, become accustomed to the light of intelligibility, will be unwilling to return (as in a return to the Cave) to the world of 'human affairs'. Glaucon thinks this is the likely outcome, but Socrates says that is the philosopher has 'any sense' (518a) he will reflect on the two causes of confusion and then see that he ought to regard those who are confused by the transition from darkness to light with sympathy and those who are confused by the return trip's transition from light to darkness should be congratulated.

In an important move for Plato, he then has Socrates give an educational mission statement: the educator cannot put learning into empty minds, any more than sight can be poured into blinded eyes: however,

> 'our argument indicates that the capacity for knowledge is innate in each man's mind, and that the organ by which he learns is like an eye which cannot be turned from darkness to light unless the whole body is turned; in the same way the mind as a whole must be turned away from the world of change until its eye can bear to look straight at reality, and the brightest of all realities which we call the good.' (518c)

Here the line that 'the capacity for knowledge is innate in each man's mind' is important: it represents a much more positive view of the human condition than some give Plato credit for.

Carrying on the mission statement for the Academy, Socrates suggests that the business of turning minds around could become a 'professional skill', a somewhat ironic point given that was long-since Plato's business. But the next point reinforces the earlier one about the innate capacity for learning, as Socrates says that the excellences of the mind, all of the skills and insights that intellect can gain, have to be cultivated and developed through training and practice, akin to developing physical skills (518d). Philosophers, he concludes, are to cultivated 'to act as leaders and king-bees in a hive' (we are, it seems, back to the bees of the Meno!), philosophers are 'better and more fully educated than the rest and better qualified to combine the practice of philosophy and politics.' Philosophers must each 'descend in turn and live with your fellows in the Cave and get used to seeing in the dark; once you get used to it you will see a thousand times better than they do and will distinguish the various shadows, and what they are shadows of, because you have seen the truth about things admirable, just and good' (520c-d).

> ## A summary of some of the key relationships in the analogy of the Cave:

THE PRISON/CAVE		THE EVERYDAY WORLD OF COMMON EXPERIENCE
Being fastened by neck and legs	REPRESENTS	The mind being trapped with a narrow range of sense experience within a world of unchallenged assumptions: the state of ignorance.
The light of the fire	REPRESENTS	The power of the sun. (An analogy within the analogy)
The ascent of the prisoner to the outside world of daylight	REPRESENTS	The upward progress of the mind via philosophical thinking towards the intelligible domain. (The ascent could be tracked on the Divided Line). The state of enlightenment
The sun	REPRESENTS	The form of good
The return of the prisoner to the Cave and the problems he faces	REPRESENTS	The role and attendant risks of being a philosopher.

KEY TERMS

deduction - induction - metaphysics - ethics - virtue - concepts - phenomena - relativism - subjectivism - forms/The Form of the Good- illusion - belief - knowledge

SELF-ASSESSMENT QUESTIONS

1. Explain why mathematics is important to Plato.

2. Explain why Plato favours discussion over writing.

3. Illustrate and explain how Plato sees the relationship between concepts and phenomena.

4. Explain the key features of the 'theory of forms'.

5. Explain what we learn about the form of the Good from the Simile of the Sun.

6. Explain what we learn about reason in the 'divided line'.

7. What is Plato's aim in the analogy of the Cave?

8. What is the role of the released prisoner in the analogy of the Cave?

9. How does Plato explain the meaning of the analogy of the Cave?

10. Make notes on the evidence you see so far to support the views that Plato a) values or b) devalues 'this life'.

FURTHER READING

- Mason (2010) Chapters 1 and 3

- Melling (1987) Chapters 1, 2, 10 and 11

- Honderich (1999) pp. 9-21

- Magee (1987) Chapter 1

- Annas (2003)

- Hare (1996)

Aristotle

(384-322 BCE)

Aristotle came as a student to Plato's Academy at the age of seventeen and he remained there until Plato's death in 347 BCE. Aristotle was not Athenian. He was born in Stagira, in northern Greece, with a strong family connection to Macedonia and to the royal family there. This lack of Athenian pedigree is probably the main reason why Aristotle did not succeed Plato as head of the Academy. Instead, after Plato's death, Aristotle left Athens and after working privately, he was invited back to Macedonia to tutor King Philip's son Alexander, later Alexander the Great.

In 335, with Alexander in the ascendant, Aristotle returned to Athens and founded the Lyceum, a centre for study. His reputation made this a success and his work there lasted twelve years during which time under Alexander the Macedonians became the dominant political force. However, when Alexander died in 323, Athenian opinion turned against anything with a Macedonian connection and Aristotle faced a charge of impiety reminiscent of the problems Socrates faced back in 399. Aristotle returned to his homeland, but he died the following year at the age of 62.

These unfortunate events at the end of Aristotle's life have an effect on our grasp of his work. His habit was to write voluminously on the subjects he was interested in note form or in brief, rather abstract essays. This material was fine as a basis for teaching, but it does not make for easy reading today. Aristotle's work, or most of that which has survived, is thus in generally much more 'esoteric' than 'exoteric' and there is a great contrast with the work of Plato. Plato's writing has real literary quality and students of classical Greek study his dialogues because of that. The same cannot be said for Aristotle. A translator of the Metaphysics remarks that the text, like Aristotle's other extant works 'might be described, with lavish generosity, as grainy'. (H Lawson-Tancred, Aristotle, 2004:xi) Jonathan Barnes describes Aristotle's' writings as 'impersonal' and their style as 'often rugged' and 'terse'. (Barnes 2000 p.1and p.5) We will see something of this when we examine some of Aristotle's own writing on the key ideas we study later on.

A real problem for Aristotle the circumstances in the last year of his life left him little time to write up his works into a more readable form. It is thought that we owe very considerable debt to his son that his writings, such as survived, were ordered and catalogued to the extent that they were.

To turn to the Metaphysics, the text is consists of fourteen sets of essays, outlines and notes and it seems likely that he wrote on the topics considered throughout his life. Aristotle never uses the term 'metaphysics' for this set of work. The title literally means 'after physics', and it may be that this title was given because those sorting his work out after his death collected the material together after they'd done the Physics. However, there is a major theme that runs through the work as stated by Aristotle:

> 'There is a kind of science whose remit is being qua being and the things pertaining to that which is per se.' (Metaphysics, 1003a)

To study 'something qua something' simply means to study something under a given heading. We might study cabbage qua biology, or qua cooking; we might consider sunsets qua Physics or qua Art History. What Aristotle means with the science that deals with 'being qua being' is that philosophy as he understands it is the study of the nature of being, by which he means the study of that which is fundamentally real (that which is 'as such' or per se). Since the time of Aristotle, the problem of substance, of what essentially is most real, is a major topic of interest in metaphysics. It is worth noting that the study of being can be seen still as the basis for theories of meaning, truth and value.

ARISTOTLE & PLATO

Aristotle was a prolific writer and a committed teacher. His major works include *Categories*, *Physics*, *Metaphysics*, *Prior* and *Posterior Analytics*, and *Nicomachean Ethics*. He held Plato in very high regard and provides important insights into Plato's life and thought. It is from Aristotle (See for example, Metaphysics 990b), that we learn that Plato, in later life, re-affirmed the importance of forms as regulative ideas with particular reference to mathematical concepts, with the concept of the Good-itself pre-eminent.

Here we find a neat and fundamental means of charting the contrast between Plato and Aristotle: for whilst Aristotle matches and in some respects exceeds Plato's comprehensive range of interests, in terms of the extent and scope of his philosophical work, Aristotle differs from Plato in a fundamental respect over the nature of the relationship between forms and everyday reality, or between the general and the particular, or, in more basic terms, between concepts and things.

For Plato, universals, concepts, i.e., the forms, and especially the form of the Good, are determinative of meaning and truth and value. The forms are regulative ideas, a domain of meaning and truth qualitatively over and above phenomenal experience.

For Aristotle, ideas (such as 'blue') or concepts i.e. forms (like 'goodness') are important and significant; but in his view they have reference to the domain of experience and to our understanding derived through our interaction with it.

Thus the concept or form 'Chair', on Aristotle's reading, has reference to and in a general sense concerns all the options for what a chair can be: but the concept 'Chair' does not denote a relation to an ideal form of 'Chairness' objectively real in a conceptual domain of generality. The same approach would be taken to the concepts of beauty, justice or goodness: all for Aristotle stand for all that in each case applies to the class of cases in question.

Let's develop our example of 'chair'.

Suppose there are ten identical chairs in a room. A Platonist would assume ten particular chairs each of which 'participates' in the overarching reality of 'Chairness' or 'the form of the Chair.'

Aristotle thinks there are ten chairs there, each of which is a case what the form of the chair is.

If we remove one chair, the Platonist does not think we have made any alteration to the objective 'form of the Chair.' But Aristotle thinks that there are now nine instances of the form of the chair in the room.

It should be clear from this example that one thing that radically distinguishes Aristotle from Plato is that for Aristotle explanations, though intellectual and reasoned, are grounded in an immanent view of 'form'. Meaning, being, value and truth are all, for Plato, determined or regulated by eternal, objective conceptual forms.

If we take our human subject, Socrates, Aristotle's view is that although Socrates through time changes in appearance and aptitude, and his moods and interests will vary and fluctuate, yet around and beneath these is a structure and organisation that is operationally constant through this process and this is the form of Socrates, an instance of human form. That Aristotelian forms have constancy is something we need to keep in mind, because Aristotle takes all matter to be eternal, an idea we will return to later.

If, for example, Socrates sits down with, say, Laura, Emily, Charlotte, Lily, Alex and Cathryn, the human Form, as Aristotle understands, is evident seven times.

But it is real and distinct in each of the seven humans.

If Socrates left the company of Laura and her five friends and disappears from view, then again, for Aristotle the form of the human in this location has reduced by one. Here again is a clear way of distinguishing Aristotle from Plato: for Plato, viewing the same group of people, the 'form of Humanity' is pure, single and conceptually prior to the existence of any so-called 'humans'. For Aristotle the 'form of Humanity' is instanced in each human.

Aristotle is sometimes characterised as an **EMPIRICIST**, as one who argues that all of our knowledge is sense-dependant. In contrast, Plato is said to be a **RATIONALIST**, one who thinks that our knowledge is mind-dependant. The problem with these tags is that they really substantially post-date the time of Plato and Aristotle, and represent later traditions of philosophical thought from the seventeenth and eighteenth centuries. By then thinkers who were consciously rationalists could trace their line of thinking back to Plato more than to Aristotle, and similarly the empiricists could claim a line of ancestry more to Aristotle than to Plato. If we use such labels uncritically of Aristotle and Plato we are likely to make some major mistakes: we might assume that Plato has no interest in science, or that Aristotle has no time for reasoning.

As it happens, Aristotle is determined to use the human capacity to reason not least with regard to concepts that can be distinct from the phenomena that are to hand. This is a vital matter, for whilst Aristotle wants to oppose the idealist trend in Plato's thought, he is just as keen to avoid falling into the materialist's camp. **MATERIALISM** was a popular view in the classical Greek world, the philosophical tradition that affirms that all of reality is an aggregate or combination of raw or basic matter or 'stuff'. Aristotle hopes to rise above this, but to do so by avoiding the signal problem that Platonists have in establishing why we must posit the objectively distinct domain of conceptual Forms.

Aristotle's Methodology

Aristotle's Metaphysics opens with the statement that 'By nature, all men desire to know' (980a). This desire stems from our intellectual faculty, 'nous' in Greek, which in modern usage has connotations of insight and natural intuition. For Aristotle this faculty operates to interrogate our experience and our ideas, to question and to seek explanations and first principles. He remarks that 'in truth nature is but one genus of that which is' (1005a); this means that 'natural science', the systematic study of nature, has a 'universal' subject matter, 'exclusively with primary substance'. Important though such a study is, and although it is kind of philosophy, Aristotle says it is not 'First Philosophy'; philosophy is always first - and underlies all other sciences.

Philosophers, Aristotle thinks, cultivate their expertise to pursue **EPISTEME**, knowledge in terms of a comprehensive and scientific understanding of the matters under review. Equipped with this outlook, Aristotle examines a wide range of topics, defining areas of study and domains of knowledge as he does so and giving us the areas of study that we now have as the curriculum of a traditional university. Aristotle maps out a scheme for what we would now term scientific enquiry, with a distinct emphasis on Biology. His philosophical interests include a number of very fundamental topics like those of substance, identity and cognition, as well as logic, ethics, political thought, argument and rhetoric and theory of poetry and literature.

It is well worth examining a bit more closely the approach or method that Aristotle usually favours in conducting an investigation; whether we would think of a scientific or philosophical or some other form of investigation, for Aristotle the method will be very much the same.

A key aspect of Aristotle's method is to attend to the 'differences' that we find in the data or in the evidence we have of the phenomenon in question. Whatever the topic or the problem, the aim will be to collate and review all of the available data, noting all the puzzles and contradictions. We seek to identify the most basic and the most regular features or concepts in relation to the data or the material we are reviewing. Through reasoning about the data, Aristotle thinks that we will get to the essence of the problem and achieve understanding of the meaning, sense and structure of the problem in question. Our process of examination will give rise to an identification of the basic principles and we will build an interpretation that constitutes an acute judgement of the matter under review, one that lays bare the truth of the matter.

Aristotle considers that in such an approach we move from the particulars that are before us and via investigation we move towards the general principles of explanation. This is now commonly termed the method of **INDUCTIVE** reasoning, the sense being that we induce or draw out the truth via the process of investigating the particulars.

One very important feature of this approach is an appreciation that what we can call 'the world', meaning 'all that appears to lie beyond us', is distinct from what we say about it. This may seem obvious, but for Aristotle the sense of the distinction here is strong and a clear motivation for the task of clarifying the ways in which we can organise our understanding to gain a better knowledge of what there is to say and know.

Again the contrast with Plato is that whereas he argues that to understand something like beauty or courage we have to abstract to the regulative ideal form, Aristotle does not think we can go beyond or behind our experience of what we can term 'this life.' Aristotle accepts that we can abstract from the particulars of experience to general ideas, of truth, beauty, goodness, blueness, triangularly, or whatever. But we do so through the capacity of human intellect within and in relation to the phenomena in question found through general experience, reflection and study. Thus Aristotle, though he rejects objective and eternal forms of the Platonic variety, is in no way abandoning a commitment to reasoning and to intellectual activity; he is heavily committed to thinking and to reasoning.

As a key summary we can suggest the following:

For Plato we might have the maxim that 'concepts (i.e. 'forms') determine reality'; for Aristotle it is more a case that 'reality is expressed through concepts (i.e. 'forms')'.

Aristotle & Intellectual Principles

We have noted the inductive aspect of Aristotle's method; we can also illustrate Aristotle's commitment to rational thought and to deductive reasoning via some of the key intellectual principles that he defines in his work.

One is the **PRINCIPLE OF NON-CONTRADICTION**. Aristotle states this as follows:

> *'It is impossible for the same thing at the same time to both be-in and not to be-in the same thing in the same respect.' (1005b)*

Aristotle thinks this a self-evident principle; thus he thinks all will agree that of same thing we cannot say that it 'both is and is-not', or as we could put it, 'a thing cannot both be and not be'. For example, a blue shirt cannot be red; a banana cannot be an oak tree. To think that something can both be and not-be at the same time is to think opposite or incompatible truths simultaneously, and that, for Aristotle, won't do.

Closely related to the principle of non-contradiction is the **LAW OF THE EXCLUDED MIDDLE**. Aristotle explains this as follows:

> *'... there can be nothing intermediate to an assertion and a denial.' (1011b)*

He says that quickest proof of this comes through the definitions of truth and falsity:

> *'... falsity is the assertion that that which is is not, or that that which is not is and truth is the assertion that that which is is and*

that that which is not is not.'

Another example would be to say that the law of the excluded middle is the rule of thought that states that between two contrary views, such as we have when we say 'either you do understand this or you do not'; logically there can be no additional third statement.

A third important intellectual principle comes through the development of the principle of **SYLLOGISTIC REASONING**. (See Prior Analytics A4 27 - A22).

This is a type of formal logical reasoning and the following example makes clear the basic idea:

1. All humans are mortal.

2. Socrates is a human.

3. Therefore, Socrates is mortal.

Syllogisms of this type have two factual premises – and it is significantly Aristotelian that they are factual: 'All men are mortal': this is the major factual premise because it makes a generic claim about 'all humans'. 'Socrates is human' is the minor factual premise as it makes a specific claim that given individual is human. From these the conclusion 'Socrates is mortal' follows as a clear and valid **DEDUCTION**; the conclusion is reasoned and the conclusion is true necessarily.

Of course, the deduction is valid and true **IF AND ONLY IF** the factual premises are both correct, and it may be that on a given occasion one or both of the premises are false.

For example:

- All men are nice.

- Hitler is a man.

- Therefore Hitler is nice.

The logic is clear here, but is the conclusion obviously true? Is the first factual premise true?

With the proviso of factual correctness in mind, we can check how Aristotle sets out the logical structure of syllogistic deduction more formally, via the innovative device of using letters instead of words. This introduction into logic of notation is a real development for which Aristotle is much credited.

In the section which follows, the first example is given in full; for the rest the first factual premise and either the conclusion or the second factual premise are given, and the exercise is to work out the logical solutions (which are given a page or so on).

1	2	3	4
All As are B	All As are B	Some As are B	Some As are B
All Bs are C	No Bs are C	? ? ? ?	All Bs are C
All As are C	? ? ? ?	Some As are C	? ? ? ?

The importance of syllogistic reasoning and the principle of non-contradiction for Aristotle is that they provide rational principles of necessity. That is to say, by means of such principles we can lay bare a pattern of reasoning where something can be exposed as following from necessity from something else. 'If p, then q: p, therefore q', for example. The principle of necessity is crucial to Aristotle's project and if we were to make a detailed review of his work we would time and again find evidence of his reasoning that given so-and-so, the conclusion follows 'of necessity'.

A fourth core intellectual procedure Aristotle employs and refines is that of the **SUBJECT-PREDICATE** relation. Aristotle develops this through his examination of the problems of substance and identity, i.e., what sort of residual 'stuff' is really in being, and in virtue of what is the identity or particularity of a given thing, state or relation known?

Aristotle (See for example Prior Analytics, A4 - A6) thinks that a sentence that expresses a basic truth-claim, a 'proposition' will have within it the 'term'; Aristotle calls the thing referred to by a proposition the 'subject' and that which is affirmed or denied of it is the 'predicate'. Aristotle's theory is that insofar as we are able to establish true predicates of a given subject, we will have established the defining qualities or characteristics of the thing in question. Thus we are able to understand and can elucidate our sense of the thing in question. The 'thing in question' is thus composed of and defined by its predicates or attributes. Aristotle distinguishes the predicates of identity from the predicates of possession, and this demonstrates a further finesse in Aristotle's intellectual method.

As an example of the points at stake, we might take Person A, and say that they have blue eyes and that they are human. It would be clear to Aristotle that being human is more fundamental that having blue eyes and that being human does not depend on having eyes that are blue, or on having eyes that work. Possessing eyes of a given colour will be a legitimate part of detailing the predicates of possession of a given subject (Person A), but if we want to articulate that persons predicates of identity we need to zone in on more fundamental predicates of identity that are expressive of that which is distinctively and generically human.

Pressing on to the more fundamental, distinctive and determinative level is precisely what Aristotle majors in. Like a great detective he always wants to hone down the patterns of evidence to find the actual core reason, sense or cause that explains and shapes the thing in question.

Solutions to the syllogisms: 2) All As are B; No Bs are C; No As are C. 3) Some As are B; All Bs are C; Some As are C. 4) No As are B; All Bs are C; Some As are C).

Aristotle on Causality

Aristotle's remark that 'By nature, all men nature desire to know' is nothing if not autobiographical. What emerges from the systematic work that Aristotle conducts is the view that **THINGS HAPPEN FOR REASONS**; things are not accidental but occur or develop because of inherent capacity or via interaction with other things. Thus his view is that we know things and understand them when we know the reasons or causes for them. A given thing is thus describable as an effect of a prior reason, cause or series of causes; this whole process is what termed 'causation'.

Let's take a couple of examples: if we considered a city (London, for example) or a forest (Sherwood) we'd find that neither 'just happens'. Cities and Forests 'are' because other things, states, or relations 'were'. Cities and forests have histories, reasons, and patterns of causal relations that provide the cumulative explanation of why and how they came to be.

In his consideration of causation, Aristotle develops some highly influential views. At one level he has what we might term a 'micro' theory to explain the reasons for things in causal terms, and this is the 'theory of the four causes': there is also a broader 'macro' explanation of the process of change which comes through the theory of change as involving a relation between what is actual and potential, which involves the actualisation of potential. We need to consider these ideas carefully.

The Four Causes

Aristotle's 'four causes' are easily stated: he considers that the explanation of any given thing will involve the material, formal, efficient and final aspects of causation. He sets out a definition of his view of the four causes in the fifth book of his Metaphysics (**NOT** Book 12 as the OCR specification suggests).

The passage is a very good example of what we noted earlier about Aristotle's writing, its 'grainy, 'rugged' and 'terse' character:

1. An intrinsic feature from which something is produced. Examples: the bronze is the cause of the statue, the silver of the salver. Also the kinds of such things are causes of them in this way.

2. The form and template, which is the account of the what-it-was-to-be-that-thing. Also the kinds of form are causes in this way. Example: the proportion of 1 to 2 and, at a more general level, number are the cause of the octave. Also the intrinsic parts of the account.

3. The source of the primary principle of change or **STASIS**. For example, the man who deliberates is the cause of action, and the father is the cause of the child. In general, the producer is the

cause of the product and the changer of the thing changing.

4. Cause as end. The end of something is what that thing is for. For example, the end of taking a constitutional is to be healthy. "Why", we might ask, "is this chap walking about the place?" "It is in order", replies the expert, "to be healthy", and in so saying he reckons to have put his finger on a cause of the behaviour.

Causes in this way are also all things which lie on the way to the end, when some other agent has initiated the process. For instance, to reach health you may have to go through dieting, purgation, medication or surgery, all of which are for the end of health'. (Metaphysics, Delta 2, 1013a-b, p115. Aristotle also sets out the four causes in his Physics, II 3)

There are a number of ideas to unpack here.

1. If we pick up on Aristotle's example of the bronze that is the cause of the statue, what he says about his in his own explanation of the passage we have quoted is that it is the 'material' cause. By this he means to say that all things have residual matter or stuff they are composed from. But Aristotle is not just a materialist, as we have explained, so material cause is but one component in his causal theory.

2. When Aristotle refers to the 'form and template' he does mean 'form' very much in the sense that we also explained earlier. This is therefore the formal cause of the thing in question; the plan, template or theory of the thing in question, and also the intrinsic nature of the thing itself.

3. We have the efficient cause; another example Aristotle gives is of the builder who has the expertise to produce a building. (See

Metaphysics 1014a)

This is a better example than his somewhat dated and biologically partial example of the father being the cause of the child.

Fourthly, the idea of cause an 'end', also known as 'final cause'. By 'end' Aristotle means the reason or point there was to the thing in question. As he says, the end is 'what that thing is for'.

If we took one of Aristotle's examples we can illustrate the four causes as follows (Metaphysics 1013a - 1013b):

1. Suppose we have a quantity of stone, timber, sand, water, cement, tools, nails; here we have the material cause for a building.

2. We have plan or design of the building from an architect, so we have the formal cause for the building.

3. We have a skilled team of builders, so we have the efficient cause for the building.

4. The point, reason or end of building the house was to have a home to live in. This is the overarching end or final cause for building a house.

Suppose that an examination question asks for an explanation of Aristotle's theory of the four causes. Showing that you know one of his examples is one way of giving an explanation. Another is to have your own worked example. This means that two worked examples which follow are merely that, examples of what you need to develop of your own to use as and when necessary.

> ▸ **Example 1: The Four Causes - Planting a Conker**

Suppose we have some conkers collected from a stroll through a wood. We might well amble home and decide to plant one in the garden. It will not be too much of a surprise if, so long as we tend the plot carefully, in due course a sapling begins to show. Within a few years, we might hope to have a strong young tree growing straight and true.

Now suppose Aristotle pays a visit, considers the young tree, and learns that we had planted the conker, what might he say to explain its development?

Aristotle first says that the growth of our Chestnut tree is due to **MATERIAL CAUSES** – the tree grows because it is composed from matter that allows this form of development. If I had planted a stone conker it would not grow as it was of the wrong matter or stuff.

Additionally, the trees may be sad to grow because of **FORMAL CAUSES**; the conker is of a distinct species, structured to allow for the growth that we now see in evidence. The structure or form as Aristotle terms it, has to be operational for anything to happen. If a conker was baked so as to prepare for the UK Conker Championships, such a conker would, after the competition, not be one that we'd get to grow. The material cause would be present, but the formal structure would be destroyed by the baking.

To material and formal causation Aristotle adds a third sense: growth comes about because of **EFFICIENT CAUSALITY**. The tree grows in response to the external structure of environment, from the moisture and minerals in the earth and from the light of the sun and from the care given.

Material, formal and efficient causality appears to give a comprehensive explanatory overview of what has caused the tree to grow. Conkers are made of matter that allows for growth and they are formally structured or organised to enable this. To these, the **MATERIAL** and **FORMAL** aspects of causality, Aristotle notes the influence of the structures around the plant that gives causality its **EFFICIENT** aspect. But Aristotle is not done; there is the final aspect to causation: by this, Aristotle means what can be called the teleological form of explanation. The term 'teleological' is taken from the Greek, **TELOS**, meaning inner aim, purpose or goal. Aristotle's point is that things, especially living things, have an inner aim or purpose that they grow towards. Living things, whether conscious, like humans, or non-conscious, as trees appear to be, exhibit a drive towards maturity or completion. This drive or purposefulness is the **FINAL ASPECT** of causality, and the aspect that sets the development and growth of the thing in question into the broadest explanatory framework.

▸ **Example 2: The Four Causes - Building a Model Plane**

Suppose Michael has been given a model plane kit. He opens the box and the kit is in many plastic parts.

Fortunately, there are instructions in the box and he has the expertise and equipment to build the kit.

He has been given the kit and has the expertise because he has been building up a collection of model aircraft, the new kit was an addition to the collection.

So in this example we have the plastic components of the kit as the **MATERIAL CAUSE**; the instructions as the **FORMAL CAUSE**; the expertise and equipment to build the kit as the **EFFICIENT CAUSE**, and the **COLLECTION** to which we wanted to add as the **FINAL CAUSE**.

With regard to the four causes a key issue is to appreciate the way that final cause relates to the other three. In everyday terms, Aristotle means that the real meaning, point or value of a process is what he has in mind for final cause. It is also important to see that he is thinking of the **FOUR CAUSES** as aspects of **ONE PROCESS**.

Thus the aim of building the house was to get a home.

The reason for planting and tending the conker was to get a mature tree.

The purpose of building the kit was to add to a collection.

In all cases, for Aristotle, the end, final causation, gives purpose and meaning to the process we go through with the first three causes: yet clearly, the end of final cause depends on the first three.

▸ **Aristotle on 'form and matter' and on Actual and Potential.**

In his view of the four causes Aristotle uses, with the first two causes (the material and the formal) one of his most famous ideas about the nature of things. This is the view that to understand things in general we need to keep in mind the dual aspects of the stuff or 'matter' from which they are composed and the structure or 'form' that they have. (See for example Metaphysics 1033b)

To take one of Aristotle's examples, if you make ball out of bronze, the bronze ball does not create roundness. The structural form of roundness is manifest in the bronze matter that is fashioned into a ball. Aristotle's anti-materialism is again in evidence here. But so is his anti-Platonism, in that he denies categorically that forms are 'substances in themselves'. He claims to have done away with the view that forms are **TEMPLATES**.

(1033b) The way in which Aristotle disposes of Plato's view of how forms determine realties is via what we termed above his 'macro theory' of the reasons for things and so for of change, which says that **THINGS COME ABOUT THROUGH THE ACTUALISATION OF POTENTIAL**.

This is something Aristotle sets out in forthright manner:

> *'… there can be no doubt that actuality is prior to potentiality.'*

> *'potentiality… is a principle of change either in some other thing or in itself qua other, but is extended, quite generally to very principle of process or stasis.'*

POTENTIALITY 'is a processing principle, through it operates not in something other that what has it but in that very thing **QUA** other.' (See Metaphysics 1049b)

Aristotle gives another example related to building which we can develop slightly: a builder en route to work has actuality as a 'builder-en-route-to work'. He has potentiality to build, but he will not realise that potentiality until he arrives at the site and begins to work.

Aristotle realises that there is an overlapping of actual and potential in species membership within a period of temporal succession. He remarks that 'every output of a production progresses towards a principle, towards an end. A principle is something for whose sake something else is, and an end is something for whose sake a production occurs. But the end is the actuality, and it is for the sake of this actuality-end that the potentiality is brought in.' (1050a)

To illustrate the point here, suppose we revisit the earlier example of the conker we planted. Our conker is actual; we can polish it, plant it or whatever. But we can't snap our fingers and magic into being what it has the potential to be, a fully-grown, mature horse chestnut tree. Our conker, planted and tended, has the potential to realise the actuality of a mature horse chestnut tree, and it has that potentiality as a part of its intrinsic nature, as its form, as Aristotle understands it. We would assume the point, the aim, the purpose, of planting a conker would be to get the actual mature tree: and a mature tree, the actualisation of the potential in the conker, would then, all being well, productive of more potentiality via the annual crop of conkers.

▸ Aristotle on Motion and First or Prime Mover

As we have seen Aristotle invests much thought on the concepts of causation, form and matter, and the relation between that which progresses from actual to potential. All of these lines of thought are subsets of a more general theory Aristotle has about reality or being. This is the view that motion or change is a fundamental characteristic of how things are, how everything is, and so how reality is to be rightly understood.

In Lambda, the twelfth book of the Metaphysics, Aristotle says the following:

> *'Our model of change is that in all cases there is (a) a thing that undergoes change, (b) something by which it is changed and (c) something into which it changes.' (Metaphysics 1069b-1070a)*

Aristotle adds that the 'something' which is responsible for change as in (b) above is 'the primary mover'. Consistent with the ideas we have been considering, Aristotle sees (a) as 'the thing's matter' and (c) as 'its form'. Aristotle means that change pervades the whole process, but the 'primary mover' has a key role as the fundamental agent of change. The 'primary mover', which can also be termed 'Prime Mover' or 'First Mover': it is important never to characterise this idea as Aristotle expresses it as 'First Cause' - this is a feature of slightly different theory of the much later scholar Thomas Aquinas (c.1224-1274).

Aristotle has more to say about the 'primary mover'. He argues that there must of necessity be such 'a kind of eternal unmoved substance,' (1071b). He reasons that if this were not so, then in the process of change, in the movement from actual to potential, everything would be destructible. If everything were destructible, then the implication is that reality as whole would be a finite system running out soon. Aristotle rejects this option: 'It is ... impossible that movement should either come-to-be or be destroyed. Movement, then, is continuous 'in the way in which time is', (1071b).

Aristotle adds several other comments to explain his idea of the eternal unmoved primary mover: harking back to his view that actuality is prior to potentiality, the eternal primary mover cannot be conceived in terms of potentiality, nor as an actual to become potential; instead, the eternal primary mover is of necessity to be conceived as **PURE ACTUALITY**:

> 'There must be a principle of such kind that its substance is activity... these substances must be without matter. For their eternity is a condition on that of everything else. They, then, must be actuality.' (1071b)

> '... there must be something that moves without being moved. This will be eternal, it will be a substance and it will be activation.' (1071b)

'But there is in fact something that moves without itself being moved, existing in activation'. (1072b)

In his explanation of these points Aristotle characterises the pattern of motion generated by the primary mover as circular, consistent with the prevailing view in Greek thought that circularly was the perfect mathematical shape. Aristotle also assumes the earth is the centre of the universe and that there are forty concentric circles around the earth in which the stars are set. The first ring of stars is moved by the second ring, and so on, and Aristotle's idea is that the Primary unmoved mover moves the fortieth rings and thus explains motion for all. This 'Prime Mover' is Aristotle's ultimate explanatory principle, and the teleological character of the process comes in again as Aristotle argues that motion is mad possible because of the primary mover is 'the object of desire' for the 'object of desire and the object of thought produce movement'. (1071a) If the primary mover is eternal and the 'object of desire' then the 'intrinsic object of thought is what is intrinsically best' and it follows, for Aristotle, that 'the intrinsic object of absolute thought is the absolutely best.' (1072b)

By degrees Aristotle moves to the view that the primary mover is to be accorded the status of divinity: 'in apprehending its object thought thinks itself. For it too becomes an object for itself by its contact with, and thinking of, its object, so that the thought and its object are one and the same.' Contemplative thought is the highest good in Aristotle's ethical pantheon, and in the purest contemplative thought we can attain, thought comes to be in possession of itself, and 'that is the divine element that thinking is believed to possess. Hence too the supreme pleasure and excellence of contemplation. If then God's well-being is forever what ours are at moments, then it is a fit object for wonder, and all the more so if it is even greater. And this last is in fact the truth.' (1072b)

Aristotle gives one more set of statements about his 'God'

> 'And God also has life; for the activation of thought is a life, and
> He is that activation. His intrinsic activation is supreme, eternal
> life. Accordingly, we assert that God is a supreme and eternal
> living being, so to God belong life and continuous and eternal
> duration. For that is what God is.' (1072b)

It would be worthwhile noting the various qualities of Aristotle's 'God' to compare with the Judaeo-Christian concept of God studied elsewhere on the OCR course.

SELF-ASSESSMENT QUESTIONS

1. Explain how Aristotle sees the relationship between concepts and phenomena.

2. Explain Aristotle's method of investigation.

3. Outline Aristotle's intellectual principles.

4. With your own original example, explain the theory of the four causes.

5. Explain - ideally with another example - why Aristotle wants the 'final cause'.

6. Explain Aristotle's ideas on actuality and potentiality.

7. Explain what Aristotle thinks about motion.

8. Explain the key ideas Aristotle has about the 'Prime Mover'.

9. Make notes on what you consider to be the strengths of Aristotle's theories.

10. Make notes on what you consider to be the weaknesses of Aristotle's theories.

KEY TERMS

'being qua being' - form - matter - causation - motion - telos - actual -potential - Prime Mover

FURTHER READING

- Barnes (2000) - Chapters 11 and 12 are especially relevant

- Allen (1970)

- Magee (1987) Chapter 2

- Honderich (1999) pp. 23-31

Plato and Aristotle: their influence on later Christian Thought

PLATO

After Plato's death the Academy continued under his nephew Speusippus (405-355 BCE) and then Xenocrates (396-314 BCE) and carried on working in the style of the later Plato, developing an academic programme in mathematics, logic, metaphysics and epistemology. Later, the Academy became a centre of sceptical thought more in keeping with spirit of the early 'Socratic' dialogues. This continued for some two centuries until under Antiochus of Ascalon (c.130-68 BCE) the Academy espoused a broader synthesis of Platonic, Aristotelian and Stoic ideas. This move marks the transition into the period of 'Middle Platonism' or 'Neoplatonism'. Amongst the key thinkers in this period we may note Philo of Alexandria (20 BCE – c.50 CE), a Hellenistic Jewish philosopher who amalgamated Platonic and other philosophical themes to Jewish ethical and theological traditions and thus provided a theoretical structure that had immense influence for early Christian thinkers. Clement (150-217 CE) and Origen (185-254 CE) are two such who embraced Neo-Platonism in their theology. This trend gives rise to the misleading view that there is a body of positive doctrine that is 'Platonic'. On the other hand, in the modern period, through the new humanism of the Renaissance in the Fifteenth and Sixteenth centuries, and the intellectual Enlightenment of the eighteenth century, there began the more careful and systematic re-reading of the Platonic dialogues that has made clear their rather less doctrinaire nature, and re-introduced the notion that it is for his method and for the range of problems he reviewed rather than for the specific theories he advanced that Plato is to be esteemed as a philosopher.

However, in the amalgamation of Platonism with theological traditions from Judaism and later Christianity key points are:

- That the logos - the word of reason - is expressed in and to the created order though that structures of nature and though human reason and intelligence, (see John 1 v1ff).

- The theological idea of a heavenly realm, sometimes referred to as 'the kingdom of God', finds conceptual expression in Plato's understanding of an intelligible domain of concepts and Forms.

- Plato's creation myth similarly relates to the creation myths in Genesis.

- The form of the Good and the creator God of Genesis are synthesised into the notion of the divine being as the pure, simple and immutable source of all wisdom, power, meaning, being, value and truth.

- The Forms are thus ideas in the mind of God.

- The 'appearance' of people and of things in general is less important than the 'real' character or essence - the soul - within. Thus there is much to link in with the Christian ethical view that the 'world to come', the kingdom, is more important than 'this world'; materialism and indeed the worlds of pleasure and sensation are in conflict with true fulfilment.

- We find much Platonic influence in later thinkers like Augustine (354-430) and Anselm (1033-1109).

ARISTOTLE

Aristotle's work was much less influential than Plato's in the emerging Christian tradition. After his death Aristotle's ideas were neglected in Western thought. Ironically, when Islam spread into the West the works of Aristotle were found and were translated from Greek into Arabic. Islamic scholars found much of interest in Aristotle's scientific writing as well as in his theories of causality which they felt was compatible with the monotheism of Islam.

In the thirteenth century, during the Crusades, Arabic copies of Aristotle's work made their way back to the West, and were translated into Latin from Arabic. Aristotle's work then had tremendous influence through the use made of it by Aquinas and by the adoption of the scientific approach within the nominalist tradition.

For both theisms, the key points are these:

- Aristotle's idea of qualitative gradation in the explanatory series of cause and effect or of motion, to an unmoved mover, ties in with the concept of the divine as supreme, as wholly 'other', and as transcending the finite universe.

- It also links to the view that reality depends on something and derives from something greater, again qualitative 'greatness'.

- The idea of God as the source of all power, meaning, value and truth has an Aristotelian aspect as well as a Platonic one.

- However, the biggest idea that Aristotle contributes for religious systems like Christianity or Islam is the teleological sense, the idea that reality has a shape or purpose, a meaning towards which it is moving and which is given by the creative impulse of the divine.

- This gives incentive to later thinkers who, following Aristotle's view that we can learn through experience and reflection on the world around us, to develop natural theology, theology based on reasoning about the world viewed as creation and as that within which divine purpose is evident. Aquinas is the most famous example of this.

Reviewing Plato and Aristotle

In the light of the study we have made of Plato's ideas, and from the consideration of Aristotle's theories, which are to some extent framed in critical dialogue with Plato's thought, this section sets out to consider some of the most emphatic criticisms that have been made against the key ideas of both thinkers. With both thinkers the aims are to illustrate and suggest lines of criticism that can be taken further through reflection and discussion, and to enable a sound basis to consider the 'strengths and weaknesses' of both.

PLATO

The Theory of Forms lies at the heart of the Platonic views we have considered

In his work from Phaedo to the Republic and in the Parmenides, Plato presents and refines the so-called 'Theory of Forms'. But it would be fair to argue that as he never gives a definitive account of the theory this could be construed as a criticism along the lines that there is no one theory to consider. It has been written that 'it is not clear that his views were really systematic enough to be called a theory' (Mason, 2010:28), and obviously this could give a neat line of criticism to develop.

Now two related questions:

1. Do we need the 'theory of Forms'?

2. Does such a theory make sense?

Suppose we accept that despite its unsystematic nature, we can say that Plato has a tangible 'theory of forms'; do we need it, and in any case, does it make sense?

There are a number of issues raised by these questions. Linguistic terms for mathematical concepts, like 'triangle', and the geometric shapes with three internal angles that we can draw with varying degrees of precision, are distinct from the Platonic form of 'Triangularity', which is an ideal, pure, objective and eternal. Plato thinks it self-evident that objective judgments must have a rational and objective base in which they participate and by which they are determined in terms of their possibility. But can we make sense of the mode of 'participation' here implied? Do we need the additional complexity of an allegedly eternal domain to make sense of rational aspects of the mind?

What is unclear to Aristotle (See for example Prior Analytics, B21:22-30) and to others since is why we can't make better sense of rational capacities by referencing them as capacities generically allied to humanity. Aristotle's view, simply put, is that we add nothing by thinking of an eternal domain of Forms over and above what we actually think. We, in the domain of appearance, actually reason, and so we don't need to extrapolate to a transcendental domain of conceptual generality to explain this. If we take a naturalistic view of what it is to be human, again a view that can be traced back to Aristotle, we could argue that we have no means by which we can, through reason, extend beyond the domain within which we reason, to see if there is something else in virtue of which all that reasoning is possible. If we reflect on entities like cabbages, receipts, textbooks, bricks and shoes, it is easy to agree through reflection on experience that we have types or sorts of things, and we can develop descriptive and definitive conceptual categories to map out the sorts of things there are. But does it make sense to envisage that this is done by and through the pre-existent and eternal Form of Cabbage, Form of Receipts, Form of Textbooks, Form of Brick and Form of Shoe? And do we have to envisage that there are actually distinct Forms for shoes as distinct as ballet-shoes and Wellington boots? Are there broad 'universals' to cover footwear in general, or are there universals for each sub-type? Plato, as we will see shortly, does not want to develop his views to cover all these cases, but the Aristotelian view is always that the 'form' of a thing will logically be that in virtue of which a particular thing or type of things is distinctly structured and organised. Thus the 'form' of the thing in question is logically intrinsic to it, not pre-existent and eternally distinct from it. Many would find this a more persuasive view than Plato's.

The Problem of the Form of the Good

In similar fashion, why do we need the Form of Good? Why can't we construct a typology of goods for the various modes of personal, social and political action that humans engage in? Plato's analogy with the sun is especially weak at this point. We can, of course, agree that within the universe of experience that is 'this life' in which we all share, we can affirm the experiential truth that the light by means of which all see derives from the one sun. The problem with the analogy of the Sun in the Analogy of the Cave (and the Simile of the Sun) can be set out as follows:

- We have a Sun, and we can explain how it is vital for the provision of light to the world of experience.

- Plato wants to use this as analogous to the Form of the Good, the absolute and objective Form which gives order and structure to all things.

- But whilst we can all agree about the Sun, the fact is that we don't agree about what is good.

- This shows that 'the Good' and 'the Sun' inhabit different and incommensurable domains:

  (a) The Sun is in the observable world of general experience and can be verified.

  (b) The idea of the 'Form of the Good' is a non-verifiable ideal.

If the reasoning here is sound then it is a conceptual error to take the Sun as an analogy for an ethical ideal, the 'Good-itself' or 'the Form of the Good'. By default we can't 'see' this; that we contest what the goods are for a given occasion is not grounds for inventing an overarching Good, it is better to establish to order of goods for the occasions that arise. What makes a good essay is distinct from what makes a good cup of coffee, which is distinct from what makes a good deed on and for a given occasion. When we say the goods are distinct here, we simply mean that each type of thing has its own specification for what is best and that is the good for the case in question. We could develop a set of criteria for a good essay, cup of coffee or a deed. Each could be distinct and clear as definitions we construct and defend. Does it not make more sense to explain the range of goods like this, without invoking the 'Form of the Good'? Can't we defend **CONTEXTUAL** or **PARTICULAR** goods without falling into loose forms of relativism or subjectivism?

Are forms so limitless as to make the theory meaningless?

As we mentioned earlier, in his dialogue Parmenides Plato sets a youthful Socrates as the defender of the theory of Forms against the aged but still alert Parmenides. Unusually it is Socrates who sets out ideas and it is Parmenides who challenges them. Through the character of Parmenides a range of criticisms against the coherence of the forms are set out. In many respects, in this dialogue Plato contributes greatly to the tradition of criticism of his own theory of Forms.

'Is there a form, itself by itself, of just and beautiful, and good, and everything of that sort?' (130b). Plato has Parmenides ask Socrates this question. Unsurprisingly, Socrates agrees there is. We know that Plato likes the idea of the distinct, objective forms and of the form of the Good. But Parmenides then asks whether there is also 'a form of human being, or fire, or water?' Socrates begins to express uncertainty as to whether these things should considered in the same way, and Parmenides then asks 'what about ... hair, mud and dirt, or anything else totally undignified and worthless?' Does each of these have distinct forms too? One might add that particulars of an even less attractive kind could be investigated. Is there a form of cancer to reference each of the various instances of cancer? We might ask about various other viral or bacterial matters. And if we were in the jaws of a great white shark somewhere off the coast of South Africa, will we have time to reflect on whether this great white is an instance of the Form of the shark, the Form of the Fish, the Form of the animal, or the Form of life?

Socrates is unwilling to allow these aggregations of Forms, and Plato may well have allegiance to his view in Republic that 'we always postulate in each case a single form for each set of particular things, to which we apply the same name.' (596a) Plato would thus reject the suggestion that every word we give to a number of cases reflects a form.

Plato would regard diseases and even sharks as parts of the visible world, and so he would not consider that the theory of Forms would be applicable. The theory of forms generally, the Forms of the beautiful, just and good and so on, are the objective ideals of the virtues. That this is what Plato wants is one thing; the snag is whether he gives a compelling reason why his theory would not apply to all sets of things, even things that are dangerous like diseases, sharks or examinations. Plato's selectivity is perhaps less persuasive than option of denying the objective reality of all forms.

The logical problem in the Theory of Forms (The 'Third Man' Argument)

Parmenides involves a logical question against the theory of forms in terms of the problem of largeness. It starts with the view that that from a number of cases of largeness, there is 'some one character' in them all from which the conclusion is that 'the large is one.' (132a) Socrates agrees this so. Plato then unleashes Parmenides with the following argument:

> 'What about the large itself and the other large things? If you look at them all the same way with the mind's eye, again won't some one thing appear large, by which all these appear large? ... So another form of largeness make its appearance, which has emerged alongside largeness itself and all the things that partake of it, and in turn another over all these, by which all of them will be large. Each of your forms will no longer be one, but unlimited in multitude.'

This criticism, which Aristotle called the 'third man argument' (See for example, Metaphysics, 990b), is regarded as one of the strongest criticisms of the theory of forms.

The suggesting is that with whatever example we choose, to make the link between the particulars in question and the form to which they are said to relate, another form of the form in question is needed to make the link, leading to a **CONSTANT AGGREGATION** of that form. To see how this criticism works it is well worth re-reading the brief quotation from Parmenides, and then the following example given by Roger Scruton should help make the key point:

> *'If individual men are men by virtue of their participation in the Form of Man, by virtue of what is the Form itself a Form of Man? Does it not have something in common with its instances (manhood), and does this not mean that both it and they participate in a further Form which determines what they have in common. In which case, are we not at the beginning of an infinite regress?' (Scruton 1994 p. 518)*

Let's take one more example, and to end of applying this to the core idea of the form of the Good, we can take the concept of goodness:

Suppose we judge that we see some aspect of 'goodness' in persons A, B and C. We thus have a 'form of goodness' in virtue of which A, B and C are deemed 'good'. If we then consider this 'form of goodness', for it to known that this participates in the form of the Good there must be another 'form of goodness' in virtue of which all of these cases of 'goodness' are correlated with the 'form of the Good'; we thus need another 'form of the Good' to account for that correlation, and so on ad infinitum.

Can Plato's theory of forms escape this criticism? Plato's view is not, of course, that the form of the Good (or any of the forms) is just a thought or mental construct. It is not his view that we get ideas of various particular goods, and then link this to an ascending web of definitions based on ideas or concepts. His theory, in the case of goodness, is that the form of the Good is **GOODNESS-ITSELF**; thus the form of the Good is not another type, level or class of goodness; it is 'goodness as such'. The form of the Good is for Plato the reason and explanation for all instances of goodness, but it is also 'good in itself'. Plato's own argument to this effect comes in Phaedo where he discussed beauty rather than goodness:

> *'It seems to me that whatever else is beautiful apart from absolute Beauty is beautiful because it partakes of that absolute Beauty, and for no other reason... the reason why a given object is beautiful... the one thing makes that object beautiful is the presence in it or association with it (in whatever way the relation comes about) of absolute Beauty. ... It is by Beauty that beautiful things are beautiful.' (99d)*

One could construct an explanation along these lines for justice-itself, courage-itself and the Good-itself. Given that Plato takes the forms in this sense to be objective and eternal he could be said to have a way of escaping Parmenides' logical criticism. But he does only in the assumption that we know what is meant by 'how the relation' of 'association' or 'presence' comes about. Plato is vague about this in the Phaedo is the passage quoted above, and he is vague about it in his work in general.

The Problem of Participation

As we have just seen, Plato's view is that which is good or beautiful or just is so because of the 'presence' or 'association' it has with the form in question. He also explains this by saying the relationship is one of partaking, of 'sharing' in (See Republic, 476d) or of 'participation' (See Phaedo 101a).

In critical discussions, a common line of criticism is to say that

1. Plato's claim is that, for example, the good of A, B and C is so because in each case the goods 'participate' in the reality of the good-itself;

2. Plato gives no convincing account of how exactly this 'participation' takes place;

3. So the claim of 'participation' breaks down.

Can we make sense of what 'participation' and the various other terms mean and forge a defence for Plato? In Parmenides (130e-131e) Socrates is challenged over whether each form is to be considered as a whole, or as something that is divisible. Parmenides' point is to establish what is happening when it is said that something that is good, for example, gets its goodness as a share of the form of the good. Socrates agrees that this sharing or partaking can only be of the form as a whole or as a part. Socrates wants to maintain they are one but Parmenides thinks this amounts to a paradox; the form of the Good is one, whole and distinct, yet it is 'in things many and separate'. How can this be? Two examples of something that can be a whole and yet be shared by many are then discussed; first of all 'one and the same day' which is one and yet in many places at the same time and is none the less not separate from itself'; secondly, a sail that we might cover many people with, so that it is both one thing and yet 'over many'.

Suppose we take our own example:

- Imagine that at a fete in a warm summer's day a sustained downpour results in eighty people sheltering in a marquee.

- The marquee is one whole entity, and let us say it is analogous to the form of dryness.

- Each of the eighty individual people in the tent is distinct, but collectively they all 'share' in the dryness of the marquee. We could just as correctly say that they 'partake' of dryness in virtue of the marquee, or that they all 'participate' in the dryness given by the marquee.

- Suppose we cut the roof of the marquee into eighty equal sections and gave one section to each of the eighty people. As an entity the marquee has been destroyed. Will the eighty people now be participating in the dryness of the marquee? No, and they may or may not now be dry given that they are each wrestling with an eightieth of the former marquees' roof.

This example demonstrates that it is coherent to speak of the many participating in the one without the one being divided, which is the option Socrates (and so Plato) defend. In our example, it would make no sense to cut up marquees to keep people dry, and it is not problematic to imagine many partaking in the shelter given by one.

This perhaps suggests that the problem of what is meant by 'participation', and the other terms used, is not so problematic after all.

But this, we argue, is not so.

The example of the tent show us what Plato wants to express, but it leads us to the real problem, which is that Plato is not talking about marquees or other physical structures, but about the various forms such as the just, beautiful and the Good. He takes the view that these are fundamentally real, objective and true. He assumes they can be thought about, analysed, talked about and written about as much as any other existent reality, like a day, a sail, or a marquee for example. But as we argued earlier with regard to the form of the Good, this begs the question; it is one thing to claim there are eternal, objective and really real forms; but do we know that they exist in themselves and are more than abstractions or ideals? We can define them as ideals, abstractions or as universals without implying that they have the objective true reality that Plato wants.

Can we know that the Forms really exist?

This problem can be explored from two distinct perspectives.

▸ The Empiricists' Critique

A very common reaction to Plato's theory of forms is to say that it 'makes no sense', or that 'there is no scientific proof for it'. These reactions get support from philosophers in the empirical tradition, such as John Locke (1632-1704), David Hume (1711-1776) and A J Ayer (1910-1989).

Empiricism gets its name from the Roman philosopher Sextus Empiricus (died c.200). The empiricist takes the view that all of our knowledge is grounded in sense-experience, what we gain though sight, touch, taste, sound and smell. On this view our ideas, thoughts and concepts are based on and built out of elements of sense-data. Experience presents us with raw data, impressions which impact upon the mind, which Locke characterises as 'white paper, void of characters' (Locke 2004 II, 1, II, p. 109). Claiming that there are no innate ideas, Locke thinks that the ideas that we assemble through reflection are composed from the data given as sense-experience; on this basis empiricists think that there can be nothing in the mind that was not first in the senses, or as Hume puts it:

> 'Reason is, and ought only to be the slave of the passions, and can never pretend to any other office than to serve and obey them.' (Hume 1978 II.3.3 p. 415)

Consequently the meaning of almost everything we say or think will be given by the experiences that confirm or verify it.

Hume promotes the idea that just two criteria can be used to establish a valid claim to truth. There is 'abstract reasoning concerning quantity or number' and 'experimental reasoning concerning matter of fact and existence.' He means what later philosophers called 'analytic' and 'synthetic' truths. Thus a truth claim can either be established by logic, as in pure reasoning, deduction or mathematics, or though scientific experimental procedures. Hume shows that metaphysical and theological claims fail both tests.

If we say, setting out Plato's view that the 'form of Good' is eternal, and put this into the following claim, 'There is a really real form of the Good that cannot not be', Hume's view would be that the truth claimed here is a) not logically self-evident, so it is not true as a matter of 'abstract reasoning' and b) it is not something we can prove through 'experimental reasoning' either. Hume's conclusion is that we should, 'Commit it then to the flames: for it can contain nothing but sophistry and illusion.' (Hume (1975) XII, III, p165)

Hume's criticisms are reinforced by Ayer. The first chapter of his Language, Truth and Logic is entitled 'The Elimination of Metaphysics'. He specifically attacks all claim akin to the thesis that 'philosophy affords us knowledge of a reality transcending the world of science and common sense,' (Ayer 1990:13). A statement that makes a truth-claim, a proposition, such as our, 'There is a really real form of the Good that cannot not be', can be true if 'some possible sense-experience should be relevant to the determination of its truth or falsehood'. If it fails this test, and is not analytically true by definition, then it is 'literally senseless,' (1990:9). Ayer would take this to be the obvious conclusion with our proposition.

The empiricist's criticism remains a popular way of attacking Plato, but is as well to appreciate that the empirical perspective faces a severe challenge to its plausibility. In his study The Blank Slate Steven Pinker argues that the view assumed by empiricists since Locke (as we saw above), that humans start as neutral 'blank slates' to be shaped by nothing but experience turns out to be false: 'The modern sciences of mind, brain, genes and evolution are increasingly showing that it is not true,' (2003:421).

For consideration is the matter of taking the time to explore how the 'modern sciences of mind, brain, genes and evolution' challenge the credibility of empiricism.

▶ Kant and Wittgenstein versus Plato

In contrast with the empiricist's critique, Plato's ideas face a challenge from another perspective suggested by Kant and Wittgenstein. Immanuel Kant (1724-1804) famously argues that we can only know the world as it appears to be, as our knowledge can only be known to be governed by the faculties of reason that we, as individual rational subjects, possess. We can imagine and speculate about how things might be 'in themselves', but we cannot have knowledge in such an enterprise. So on this basis we have no justification in talking about 'essences or 'forms'. Ludwig Wittgenstein (1889-1951), in his later writings, operates on the principle that 'the meaning of a word is its use in a language', where languages are composed of dynamic 'language-games' within and as the socio-historical context for thinking and being. This entails a much more relativistic view than Plato's theory permits. The question of meaning is for Wittgenstein, prior to the question of truth. Thus his view attacks the assumption that values require absolute value, goods the absolute good - and so on, and gives a plausible alternative view. (Kant's ideas are famously set out in **CRITIQUE OF PURE REASON**, 1781. Wittgenstein's later philosophy as alluded to here is in his **PHILOSOPHICAL INVESTIGATIONS**, 1953).

So does Plato make a false inference in his arguments for the existence of Forms? Plato thinks that we can't make sense of the judgments we make of truth, beauty, justice, goodness and the like, without reference to the objective reality of the eternal Forms. Plato seems to assume that a term, to be significant, must have a referent. This or that specific 'truth' is not a sufficient referent for 'Truth', but 'The form of Truth' would be. But if we accept Kant's strictures on what we can claim to know, and apply Wittgenstein's view of language to contextualise 'truth' to the types and contexts of usage, we could argue against Plato that 'truths' are contextual and relative to use, and that a given 'truth' about a matter will be the sum total of the contributory points: 'Truth' about x is the sum total of the known cases of 'truth' about x'.

Approaches like this defend the validity of particular truth claims and allows for contrasting domains of truth relative to contrasting domains of experience; so 'truth' in Economics, 'truth' in Meteorology, and so on. We also avoid recourse to the speculative domain of 'Truth', the domain of forms, which, as we have indicated above, we would have extreme difficulty in verifying in a fashion akin to the existence of the sun.

False Analogies with Mathematics

With Plato we might agree that mathematical and logical systems which allow rational certainty are one thing. But moral and aesthetic notions like 'Goodness' and 'Beauty' are another. Linguistic terms for social and cultural experiences are not of the same order as logical systems - and logical systems can be explained as expressive features of what it is to be an evolved and genetically refined human without appeal to a metaphysical domain of regularity (such as the theory of Forms or the form of the Good). Mathematical concepts have rational purity; Plato thinks that this is analogous to the moral purity that he wants to find and express in the Form of the Good. Sauce for the logical Goose is Sauce for the moral Gander? But again, the inference or analogy is false. Moral concepts are not of the same order as logical concepts. The mathematics used to plot the trajectory of a missile will rely on logical constants that the moralities of war seek vainly to establish.

Plato thinks that in this world we find evidence of contrasting degrees of 'the good', variations of 'courage', and competing views of 'beauty' and so on. To resolve the conflicts he posits the notion of Forms and develops the view of an objective domain of forms with the 'form of the Good' as the determinative Form. But perhaps he has taken a mistaken path to solution of the initial problem. Perhaps it is wiser for the philosopher to reflect on the ongoing disputes about 'What is Good' and work on to the conclusion that this might be due to a mistaken assumption that there is a knowable 'good'. Perhaps the truth is that 'The Good' is a fiction, and the truth is that values are simply compound terms for positive feeling; values on this view might not merely be subjective, emotive and contingent, but rather natural, social and cultural, but not theoretical and objective. This is the view we might take were we to follow an Aristotelian approach to the matter.

Pragmatic Uses for the Good

Picking up a suggestion from the last paragraph, another line of criticism of Plato comes from the philosopher and novelist Iris Murdoch (1919-1999).

Her ethical perspective draws strongly on both Plato and Aristotle. Murdoch writes with a strong sense of respect for aspects of the classical tradition in philosophy. No less than Plato and Aristotle she thinks there is significant value in pursuing the question 'How can we make ourselves morally better?' (1970:52).

By writing of what 'We' and 'ourselves' might do here, she is suggesting that moral philosophy must be realistic in respect of human nature, on the basis that human nature has 'certain discoverable attributes' that the moral philosopher should consider. Here she is allied to the Aristotelian and modern traditions of virtue theory, (see p. 78). She also claims that since an 'ethical system cannot but commend some kind of ideal' it should at least ensure that it 'commends a worthy ideal.' Here she is drawing on the Platonic tradition.

She suggests a two-fold tension within which human life is led, and again, her view is that this covers human life from ancient or classical times to the present. On the one hand we are 'historically determined', 'relentlessly looking after' ourselves; we are 'largely mechanical creatures, the slaves of relentlessly strong selfish forces', the 'nature of which we scarcely comprehend,' (p. 78 and p. 99). On the other, we have the world around us, 'aimless, chancy, and huge' (p. 100). Living within the tension of these gives ethical thought the imperative task to find a way to 'make ourselves morally better'.

Murdoch does not want to defend a theological ethic, nor a view that unqualified in its support for Plato's theory of the form of the Good. But she argues that alternative ideological substitutes for the ultimate have demonstrably failed - Reason, Science, History, the Will (p. 79f). She thus favours the use of the idea of the Good which 'should be retained' as 'a central point of reflection' (p. 69).

Murdoch notes that we might consider that there are a multiplicity of distinct values or 'goods' (see p. 56 and p. 6). This can be said to militate against any claim that there is one over-arching Good. Yet there is also everyday evidence of people wanting 'perfection', 'certainly 'or 'goodness 'in their various activities'. The whole way of expressing this aspiration suggests to Murdoch a sense of a 'transcendent' Good (p. 69) of which apprehension will always be 'partial' (p. 31). She therefore argues that the Good is and will remain 'indefinable and non-representable' (p. 42) in character. However, 'The image of the Good as a transcendent magnetic centre seems to me to be the least corruptible and most realistic picture for us to use in our reflections upon the moral life.'

This argument is termed 'pragmatic' because of the reasoning which suggests that i) we habitually live by some values or other, ii) that we are inclined to follow values or ideologies that are seriously flawed, so that iii) the ideal of the Good, as a distinct theoretical value, offers the least vulnerable and more practical guide to our moral life.

Criticising Plato's analogy of the Sun in relation to the Good in the Republic, Murdoch explains that the idea is that the good man is eventually able to focus on the form of the Good, analogous to being about to look directly at the sun. Murdoch rejects this (p. 70) for the very obvious reason that the sun is something that is visible, whereas 'the Good' is not. Of better use she thinks, is the view we can take from Plato that light of the sun that enables sight is analogous to the influence of the Good that allows us to 'see things 'morally 'as they really are.'

> 'An increasing awareness of "goods" and the attempt, (usually only partially successful) to attend to this purely, without self, brings with it an increasing awareness of the unity and interdependence of the moral world.' (p. 101).

Murdoch suggests that a kind of 'contemplation of the Good' is of value, not just because it might help us to work our better ways or acting in a morally assured manner, but because it involves 'an attempt to look right away from the self towards distant transcendental perfection.' (p. 101) Such a turning away from 'the particular' is, she argues, of benefit, by diminishing of the drive of the self.

Murdoch is not defending Plato uncritically. She defends a revised Platonism with the Good as 'a worthy ideal.'

ARISTOTLE

Aristotle is open to a number of criticisms.

The Problem of Material Cause

Suppose we take example to show the four causes, and suggest that for a cake we have as the material causes the raw ingredients like flour, butter and eggs, aren't we always assuming the actuality of these material causes? If we follow Aristotle's maxims that everything happens for a reason and nothing by chance, shouldn't we in fact be analysing the material causes as phenomena that are themselves ends of a prior teleological process? Aristotle would doubtless not see this as a major challenge to his general view. He would almost certainly accept that his analysis could be refined to accommodate the idea that whilst in a given example illustrate the theory of the four causes, material cause or causes will be assumed, the analysis could be applied to the a consideration of the material causes in question as final causes of a teleological process.

A Problem from Mathematical Truth

Aristotle is emphatically opposed to the Platonic reliance on an objective but transcendent domain of forms, of concepts, in virtue of which knowledge and understanding have truth and validity. Aristotle argues for the world as known through reflection on experience as the basis for all that we can know. Platonists ancient and modern and others dispute this, with particular reference to mathematical regularities. In much more recent times empiricists have not been able to convince many that the truths of '2+2=4' are grounded in the number of cases of our finding that '2+2=4', as opposed to the rationalist and Platonic view that the truths here have a logical and necessary character that would be true irrespective of the number of times we were to count. This leads to the view that Aristotle has not refuted the possibility of truth being grounded in an abstract domain of invariability.

Criticism from Science

Aristotle's metaphysical analysis involves the view that everything happens in a sequence or structure of cause and effect, that everything is moved by a prior mover, and that everything develops from actuality to potentiality in fulfilment of its inner aim or telos. This view is hotly disputed, perhaps ironically, by later developments in science.

For example, we might consider the ideas of Isaac Newton (1642-1727). In his Principia Mathematica of 1687 he formulated three laws of motion:

1. 'Every object persists in its state of rest or uniform motion in a straight line unless it is compelled to change that state by forces impressed on it.'

    This usually called the 'law of inertia'. If you stand in at the head of a snooker table with all the balls in place to start a game, you will have an example of inertia.

2. 'Force is equal to the change in momentum (mV) per change in time. For a constant mass, force equals mass times acceleration.' $F=m\,a$.

    This, the second law of motion, is Newton's law of acceleration. The key idea is that a force applied to an objects mass (m) equals the rate of change in its momentum. You could demonstrate this law each time you cue off at the snooker table, so long as you reset the table the same way each time and you vary the force of your cue action, increasing it each time.

3. 'For every action there is an equal and opposite reaction.'

    This third law of motion says that there is always a reactive force to any force applied to an object. Imagine you break off at the start of snooker frame and strike the white ball very firmly into the pack of reds: the force of the impact will, according to Newton, be proportionally matched by the opposite reactive force back onto the white ball and/or dissipated via other reds. Another example is the moment you step out of untethered rowing boat onto dry land.

It is not hard to see what Newton's laws do to Aristotle. There is inertia, so motion is neither constant nor eternal; motion can be of the reciprocal action and equal and opposite reaction type, which leaves no room for telos or final cause. (On Newton see Gleick 2003)

Another line of scientific investigation antagonistic to Aristotle's views comes from Charles Darwin (1809-1883). In the 1830s Darwin spent five years on HMS Beagle on its mission to chart and map the coastlines of South America. During this voyage Darwin made observations, inferences and deductions that led to the view that species changed because of random variations that proved favourable when circumstances in the struggle for life altered. He concluded that species habitually bred to produce more offspring than can be supported by the resources, and that random variations that were favourable were passed on through genes which gave a better chance of survival. Darwin has these, the key ideas of natural selection, clear by about 1838. It was not until 1859 that the ideas were published in The Origin of Species:

'As many more individuals of each species are born than can possibly survive; and as, consequently, there is a frequently recurring struggle for existence, it follows that any being, if it vary however slightly in any manner profitable to itself, under the complex and sometimes varying conditions of life, will have a better chance of surviving, and thus be naturally selected. From the strong principle of inheritance, any selected variety will tend to propagate its new and modified form.' (2009:14)

Here Darwin alludes to the term 'natural selection', his name for the theory he advanced. And we see the references to the 'struggle for existence' and the variations that might give a better chance of natural selection. This view refutes the idea that there is purposeful or intentional design of the teleological kind that is in Aristotelian thought - and later on in Aquinas' natural theology. In response, those who seek to defend teleological interpretation invoke the potential inherent in a given species for progressive or developmental change, and champion ideas of intelligent design. This is an ongoing area of debate.

The Problem of Determinism: The Existential Challenge

Aristotle's views imply that the motion of things from actual to potential state and that the explanation of development through the four causes reflects that everything happens for a reason and for a purpose. On motion Aristotle remarks that 'Nothing, in fact, will be moved by chance'. (Metaphysics 1071b) If this applied to human life, one line of thinking is that the implication is that humans must live in accordance with their nature, aiming to fulfil the actualisation of their potential. It seems that as Aristotle might say, 'all humans are humans', but this suggests that we must all conform to what it is to be human. This view, a type of ethical naturalism, can be seen as the thin end of the wedge of determinism, the view that everything is shaped, conditioned and caused by prior conditions. This can be argued to distort what is qualitatively distinct about being human. The existentialist Jean-Paul Sartre (1905-80) gives a strong challenge against the idea that humans possess a 'human nature', a 'conception of human being ... found in every man'. This implies that 'each man is a particular example of a universal conception, the conception of Man', (2007:29).

For Sartre the deadly implication of such views is that the essence of what it is to be human precedes a person's unique existence, and this leads him to his alternative view that the 'human reality' is one where 'existence precedes essence', (see pp. 27-33). Sartre thinks that human life is, for each individual, freely given or gratuitous. There are no prior 'essences', so we are simply what we will ourselves to be:

Man, says Sartre, 'is nothing less but what he makes of himself', 'something which propels itself towards a future and is aware that it is doing so', 'a project which possess a subjective life'.

In one of his more famous lines, Sartre says that man 'cannot find anything to depend on either within or outside himself. He discover ... he is without excuse. For if indeed existence precedes essence, one will never be able to explain one's action or reference to a given and specific human nature; in other words, there is no determinism-man is free, man is freedom', (p. 38).

Sartre thinks that if we abdicate the responsibility of this freedom and live in conformity with an unthinking obedience of custom, habit, or convention, then we act in 'bad faith'. Sartre explicitly means to distinguish what we are as humans in terms of our physical disposition, about which we have no choice, from what we can be through act and choice, by means of which we become 'authentic'. This view assails the Aristotelian notion of things having, by their nature, the potential to be this or that. This view sounds to Sartre like a mode of determinism and he is determined to oppose it! Things may have a determinate nature and exist 'in-themselves', but humans have, through the power to choose, the ability to exist in the mode of the 'for-itself', freely and authentically.

Whitehead and the Fallacy of Misplaced Concreteness

This next criticism suggests that Aristotle's view is based on a diagnostically inconsistent solution. The English philosopher A.N. Whitehead (1861-1947) employs the phrase 'the fallacy of misplaced concreteness' to describe the way in which both Aristotle and later Aquinas provide a metaphysical review in which the key patterns to emerge are of motion, process, change, contingency, dependency and the like. Then, in marked contrast and as the alleged explanation we have the 'unmoved mover', the uncaused cause' the 'necessary being' or whatever. In other words, everything is in process but to explain this we invoke something fixed or, as Whitehead puts it, concrete. His point is that it is incoherent to invoke something so unlike that which we seek to explain as the logical or reasonable explanation. A more reasonable and much more logical explanation will be in line with the view that best solution is invariably the simplest one consistent with the evidence. Thus he argues (see 1979 p. 7 and p. 18) for reality to be a process. The Platonist might go some way to agreeing with Whitehead that the reality that we know and experience is a process of change - but still want to reason for truths (and pretty concrete ones at that) over and above or, more correctly, prior to the world of experience. This is another area of ongoing debate! However, from Whitehead and from many other critics, the view emerges that the idea of an 'uncaused cause' or an 'unmoved mover' as a characterisation of God is open to criticism as being a problematic. If everything is caused by something and if nothing can be the cause of itself, it is contradictory to then define something that is the cause of itself as the cause of all.

Aristotle imagines that 'God', the Prime Mover, must be immaterial since that which is material is subject to change, and necessarily existent or eternal, or again God would be subject to change. Thus the mode of divine being must, Aristotle suggests, be spiritual and intellectual, it must be pure thought. God is 'thinking about thinking', Aristotle thinks. The big problem with this is that begs the question as to how pure thought can act to bring things about. As Whitehead's line of criticism has it, if all of our experience through reflection on experience tells us that things move through processes of change and development and interaction, we have no experience at all to suggest that pure thought can have material outcomes. Thus the progressive argument favoured by Aristotle, from motion to a Prime Mover breaks down.

FURTHER READING

Criticism of Aristotle and Plato as reviewed in this Chapter can be pursued via the various writers and texts cited in the text. Mason (2000), Melling (1987), Allan (1970), Barnes (2000) and Magee (1987) all offer valuable lines of discussion.

AS-STYLE QUESTIONS

OCR's examination question for the current AS have a two-part structure as in the example below:

    a)   Explain Plato's theory of Forms. (25)

    b)   'Plato's theories devalue human life.' Discuss. (10)

Part a) is test of assessment objective AO1, knowledge and understanding. Part b) tests AO 2, evaluation and the ability to justify views through reasoned argument.

The Philosophy of Religion paper will have four questions on it, all in this two-part structure.

Questions on Plato and/or Aristotle may or may not appear on a given paper; but the topics have been examined regularly.

Below a series of questions in the OCR AS style:

    a)   Explain Plato's Analogy of the Cave. (25)

    b)   'Plato's theories devalue the physical world.' Discuss. (10)

a) Explain Plato's theory of Forms. (25)

b) 'There is no real evidence to justify the theory of Forms.' Discuss. (10)

a) Explain the role of the Sun in Plato's Analogy of the Cave. (25)

b) To what extent are Plato's theories convincing? (10)

a) Explain the concept of Ideals in Plato's philosophy. (25)

b) 'Without ideals our lives would be limited.' Discuss. (10)

a) Explain what Aristotle meant by Prime Mover. (25)

b) 'Aristotle's theories fail as a description of reality.' Discuss. (10)

a) Explain Aristotle's theory of the four causes. (25)

b) 'Aristotle's explanation of how things come to be is convincing'. Discuss. (10)

Questions on Plato might focus on any part of the analogy of the Cave: as in the specification, 'the prisoners, the shadows, the cave itself, the outside world, the sun, the journey out of the cave and the return to the prisoners'. How far any of these parts is an accurate portrayal of the human condition is a vital issue to consider, not least with specific reference to Plato's own explanation of the reason for and meaning of the analogy.

Questions on Aristotle could ask for a comparison between the Prime Mover and the God of classical theism, between Prime Mover and God as Creator.

Bibliography

1. Works of Plato and Aristotle

- **ARISTOTLE** - (1989) Prior Analytics, Translated et al by R Smith, Hackett, Indianapolis

- **ARISTOTLE** - (2004) Metaphysics, Translated and introduced H Lawson-Tancred, Penguin, Harmondsworth

- **PLATO** - (2005) Meno and Other Dialogues (Charmides, Laches, Lysis) Translated et al by R Waterfield, Oxford

- **PLATO** - (1969) The Last Days of Socrates (Euthyphro, Apology, Crito, Phaedo). Translated and introduced by H Tredennick, Penguin, Harmondsworth

- **PLATO** - (1996) Parmenides, Translated by M L Gill and P Ryan; introduced by M L Gill, Hackett, Indianapolis

- **PLATO** - (1973) Phaedrus and Letters VII and VIII, Translated and introduced by W Hamilton, Penguin, Harmondsworth

- **PLATO** - (2005) Protagoras and Meno, translated by A Beresford with an introduction by L Brown, Penguin, Harmondsworth.

- **PLATO** - (2007) The Republic, (2nd Edition), Translated D Lee and introduced by M Lane, Penguin, Harmondsworth

- **PLATO** - (1987) Theaetetus, Translated with an Essay by R Waterfield, Penguin, Harmondsworth

- **PLATO** - (2008) Timaeus and Critias, Translated D Lee, revised and introduced T J Johansen, Penguin, Harmondsworth

2. Secondary Texts

- **ALLAN, D.J.** - (1970) The Philosophy of Aristotle, OUP, Oxford

- **ANNAS, J.** - (2000) Ancient Philosophy. A Very Short Introduction, OUP, Oxford

- **ANNAS, J.** - (2003) Plato. A Very Short Introduction, OUP, Oxford

- **AYER, A.J.** - (1990) Language, Truth and Logic, Penguin, Harmondsworth

- **BARNES, J.** - (2000) Aristotle. A Very Short Introduction, OUP, Oxford

- **GLEICK, J.** - (2003) Isaac Newton, Fourth Estate, London

- **HARE, R. M.** - (1996) Plato, OUP, Oxford

- **HUME, D**. - (1978) A Treatise of Human Nature, (2nd edition Selby-Brigg/Nidditch), OUP, Oxford

- **HONDERICH, T.** - (ed) (1999) The Philosophers: Introducing Great Western Thinkers, OUP, Oxford

- **KANT, I.** - (1929) Critique of Pure Reason Translated by N Kemp

Smith, Macmillan, London

- **KENNY, A.** - (2010) A New History of Western Philosophy, OUP, Oxford

- **LOCKE, J.** - (2004) An Essay Concerning Human Understanding, Edited and introduced R Woolhouse, Penguin, Harmondsworth

- **LOWES DICKENSON, G.** - (1947) Plato and His Dialogues, Penguin. Harmondsworth

- **MAGEE, B.** - (1987) The Great Philosophers, BBC, London

- **MASON, A.** - (2010) Plato, Acumen, Durham

- **MELLING, D.** - (1987) Understanding Plato, OUP, Oxford

- **MURDOCH, I.** - (1970) The Sovereignty of Good, RKP, London

- **MURDOCH, I.** - (1978), The Fire and the Sun: Why Plato banished the Artists, OUP, Oxford

- **ROWE, C. J.** - (2003), Plato, Bristol Academic Press, Bristol

- **SCRUTON, R.** - (1994), Modern Philosophy. An Introduction and Survey, Sinclair-Stevenson, London

- **WHITE, N. P.** - (1979) A Companion to Plato's Republic, Hackett, Indianapolis

- **WITTGENSTEIN, L.** - (1953), Philosophical Investigations Translated by E Anscombe, Blackwell, Oxford

Postscript

Stephen Loxton is a graduate of the Universities of Sussex and Hull and is Head of Theology and Philosophy at Sherborne Girls School, where he is also Theory of Knowledge Coordinator for the International Baccalaureate. He teaches AS Philosophy of Religion and Ethics and A2 New Testament and Ethics as well as Philosophy within the I.B. programme. He holds advanced degrees in Philosophy and Theology as well as an M.Phil from Hull University.

A personal note: My deep thanks to Peter Baron for inviting me to write this book and for his support in bringing it to completion. My thanks to Jonathan Casley, Head of History of Art at Sherborne Girls, Kathryn Hall, Head of Religious Studies at Benenden School, and Samuel Loxton, for comments and feedback on early drafts of the book - all much appreciated.

This book is dedicated to my children: Joanna, Samuel, Christabelle and Reuben.

Further source material is to be found online online at:

www.philosophicalinvestigations.co.uk